MUSIC
ON A
MISSION

MUSIC
ON A
MISSION

THE STORY OF KIDLINKS

Larry V. Dykstra

Kravitz & Sons
INNOVATORS IN PUBLISHING, MARKETING AND ADVERTISING

Kravitz and Sons LLC
204 E Arlington Blvd. Suite B
Greenville, NC 27858

Published by Kravitz and Sons LLC.

ISBN: 979-8-89639-416-7 (sc)
ISBN: 979-8-89639-415-0 (e)

Library of Congress Control Number: 2025918586

DEDICATION

This book is dedicated to the more than 450,000 severely and chronically ill children and their caregivers for whom the KidLinks team has provided therapeutic music over the past forty years . . . and to the millions of others they haven't yet been able to reach.

Table of Contents

FOREWORD

The Soft-Spoken Man in the Corner
Noel "Paul" Stookey of Peter, Paul and Mary

I felt sorry for the guy, although he seemed relaxed and not the least bit upset that the mostly disinterested crowd milling around the post-concert buffet table, putting slices of cheese on crackers and balancing plastic glasses of punch and chocolate chip cookies in their hands, were ignoring the sound of his guitar and voice.

I'd been spoiled—performing with Peter and Mary on stages and in venues around the world—singing to folk music fans who were there to listen. They would come to a concert not just for the entertainment or the sense of community that a sing-along might provide, but for the message: the musical articulation of a common contemporary concern.

It is 1985, and I'm in Texas with the Bodyworks Band, a group of musicians I have been working with for almost fifteen years. We've been on the road for a week or so, and as much as we enjoy each other's company and the spiritually based songs we perform, we have families and friends waiting for us back east. I am hoping this meet-and-greet won't last too long and we can grab a few hours of sleep before showing up at the airport to head home.

"Nice guitar work!" I say as he finishes a song and I nibble on the corner of a brownie. "I'm afraid I couldn't hear much of the lyric with all the talking going on. Probably a little discouraging," I continue, "especially if you're playing something original."

He looks up and smiles. "Oh, that's not why I'm here," he says. "I volunteered to play tonight—kind of counting on the fact that eventually you'd come over and say hello." I'm a little surprised at his comment, but then he continues, "I could tell you were the kind of guy who would try and make me feel better about nobody listening." We both laugh, and then he offers his hand.

"I'm Jim Newton, and I'd like to arrange a time to talk with you about a musical project."

And that's the way it began. Within three months I had become part of a dedicated musical crew—including Jim, Paul G. Hill, and Denny Bouchard—playing, producing, and recording songs for a constantly expanding KidLinks musical library.

In these past forty years I've learned a lot from Jim and his team about music's healing power. As so often happens in the best situations, his leadership has been as much by example as declaration. Jim and his wife, Melissa, have welcomed me into their home and their family, and by virtue of their openness and caring, they demonstrate those very principles that continue to inform the KidLinks music: songs that are comforting, assuring, and for the most part designed for children. But they have adult appeal as well.

Our recording sessions are occasionally just plain goofy—and I don't mean just the music! At unpredictable intervals, the Newt might lay on a thick Texas accent, badly mispronounce a Spanish word, or put a drum cymbal on his head (particularly appropriate if the worries of the moment are oppressive and counterproductive) to remind us of our human condition . . . and connection.

But that's just the story of my involvement. I'm guessing your personal connection may begin with the heartfelt stories contained in this book. Or perhaps the story of your involvement has already begun, listening to the Foreword music in the car or reverberating (accompanied by laughter and participation) through the corridors of children's hospitals all over the world. The songs that Jim and Paul have either created or chosen to perform are songs that focus on our mutual well-being, delivered in a language that speaks with a sense of respect to the child within each of us.

Read then, be inspired, and listen with your heart.

Noel Paul Stookey
Ojai, California
March 2022

PREFACE

I wrote this book for two equally important reasons: first, to celebrate the fortieth anniversary of a nonprofit organization dedicated to bringing the healing power of music to severely ill children; and second, to honor Jim Newton, who—through his tireless passion and dedication to the cause— offers a striking example of what it means to be a servant. My deepest hope is that by understanding the origins, purpose, and contributions of KidLinks, others will be inspired to use their energies and gifts to serve others and make this world a better place to live.

This book was made possible through the financial support of the following individuals and organizations whose backing offers testimony to the belief many hold regarding the importance of KidLinks and its mission.

Charlotte and Fred Ball

Ann and JW Brown

Lyle Eastham

Aimee and Adam Hall

Georgia and Marc Lyons

Musical Hugs, LLC

Pillar Oil and Gas, LLC

Jan and Trevor Rees-Jones

INTRODUCTION

We build on foundations we did not lay
We sit in the shade of trees we did not plant
We drink from wells we did not dig
This is as it should be.

Rev. Peter Raible (1930–2004)

The opening lines of Rev. Raible's expansion of Deuteronomy 6:11 remind us that every organization, large or small, was built on the shoulders of those who came earlier. Yet organizational memories can fade with transitions and time, allowing our connection to history to slip away. Rev. Raible might agree that this is *not* as it should be.

I was fortunate during my career to work on consumer brands with rich histories, most notably Gatorade and Pizza Hut. I made it a priority to understand their roots—the people involved, the circumstances that inspired their beginnings, and the events and decisions that molded them as they grew. I believe knowing how early leaders responded to challenges they encountered reveals the stuff that defines the heart and soul of any enterprise.

Gatorade was developed in the 1960s in response to a simple question asked by a University of Florida football coach: "Why aren't my players urinating after our practices or games?" At the time, liquids were denied to athletes during workouts for fear that drinking would cause cramping. When the Florida Gators varsity team began drinking the concoction developed by Dr. Robert Cade, assistant professor at the college of medicine, their opponents came to fear and covet the magic elixir only they possessed. Gatorade was cloaked with mystique because it was created in the laboratory and proven on the playing fields. Over time, Dr. Cade's invention improved active thirst hydration practices, revolutionized sports science, and enhanced athletic performance. Rights to Gatorade were eventually sold to corporations, which made the product widely available to consumers, demonstrated the product's efficacy through visible product presence on the sidelines of professional teams, and pursued product and packaging innovations to enhance mainstream appeal. Gatorade is now available in over eighty countries and remains the leading brand in the nearly $20 billion worldwide sports and energy drink market.

In 1958, Dan and Frank Carney borrowed $600 to open the first Pizza Hut restaurant in Wichita, Kansas. The brothers were inspired by an article in the national weekly magazine the *Saturday Evening Post* that reported high unmet demand for pizza across the country. Thousands of American troops stationed in Italy during World War II had fallen for the dish but were unable to find it outside US cities with large Italian immigrant populations. The small brick building the Carney brothers bought to house their first restaurant was adorned by an outdoor sign with only enough space to paint "pizza" and a three-letter word. The franchise helped kick-start pizza's journey toward becoming America's favorite food. Today, there are Pizza Huts in 120 countries with global sales at nearly $13 billion.

Gatorade and Pizza Hut were rooted in modest expectations yet blossomed into iconic brand status. Knowledge of how each was tested and tempered over time fueled my emotional attachment to the brands. Stories of their origins connected me to something much bigger: a set of bedrock values I could apply into the future. I believe this kind of historic grounding can enrich anyone working in any organization.

The goal of this book is to share the history and values of a nonprofit organization that has quietly made a difference in the world one song and one child at a time. Jim Newton's visit to a children's hospital in 1983 moved him to establish a nonprofit—currently known as KidLinks—with the mission of bringing the healing power of music to severely ill children everywhere. Over the past forty years, with the help of others like his colleague Paul G. Hill and folk icon Noel "Paul"

Stookey (of Peter, Paul and Mary), Jim has dedicated his time and talents to developing a unique repertoire of songs containing messages these children need to hear and to bring them directly to hospitals across the country.

In 2015, Hugworks merged with the KidLinks Foundation, a nonprofit founded in 2001 by Texas energy entrepreneur J. W. Brown to raise funds to support therapeutic music training and treatment through programs like Hugworks. Bringing together these two successful charities leveraged their complementary competencies and talents: the therapeutic music resources of Hugworks and the business acumen of the KidLinks Foundation. Operating under the name KidLinks, the new organization has pursued its mission of "linking kids to healing, hope, and happiness through music and media." While they continue to record new songs of healing, KidLinks is identifying innovative ways to provide healing musical experiences for children in ways that extend far beyond what Jim could have imagined in 1983. (For more information, visit www.KidLinks.org.)

I offer this book in appreciation of Jim Newton and Paul G. Hill for their coaching and caring, which has blessed me beyond measure. I also wish to express my gratitude to the KidLinks leadership team, most notably J. W. Brown and Adam Hall, for their support of this book project.

My hope is that the story about Jim's initial motivations and unwavering pursuit of his mission will continue to inspire all who become connected to KidLinks in the future as they create new and meaningful ways for children to experience the healing power of music. For those who, as a result of this work, learn about KidLinks for the first time, I offer these closing lines of Rev. Raible's poem as a reminder of why this story matters:

Together we are more than any one person could be.
Together we can build across the generations.
We are ever bound in community.
May it always be so.

THE INSPIRATION

CHAPTER ONE

This Might Be Where I Belong

The door cracked open like a stage curtain, and Jim Newton stepped out of the elevator into the harsh glare of fluorescent lights. After more than a decade of performing in venues ranging from smoky bars to silent chapels, he suddenly felt unprepared. For the first time in years, perhaps in his life, Jim was unnerved at the thought of performing.

Jim studied his arriving audience—twelve children under the age of ten accompanied by parents and nurses moving into the common area on the fifth floor of Columbus Children's Hospital in Columbus, Ohio. (Columbus Children's Hospital officially became Nationwide Children's Hospital in 2007.) A couple of patients rode in on wheelchairs. Another lay in a hospital bed that had been pushed into the area. Casts and bandages on a few reminded Jim of a small ragtag army returning from an unsuccessful campaign. Jim smiled at the child nearest him, but only sunken dark eyes reflecting the battle being waged against his illness stared back. *How did I get myself into this?* he wondered.

*****

Jim had arrived in Ohio's capital a couple of days before to lead a spiritual growth weekend for teens throughout the greater Columbus area. Frank Luchsinger, youth pastor at North Broadway United Methodist Church, was hosting the event on the second weekend of March 1983. Pastor Frank had seen Jim the year before as the featured attraction at a youth rally and appreciated his ability to make religion relevant in the changing world of the early 1980s.

Pastor Frank wanted his teenagers to grow up with a resilient faith and to not be thrown by the difficult experiences we all face along the way. "It's just the way life is," he would tell them. "Everyone faces speed bumps and gets jolted by them. But that doesn't mean God is turning away from us or causing the pain. When the speed bumps come, our faith sustains us. Every life includes speed bumps. It's the way life is. But a resilient faith overcomes life's challenges and we experience God's nearness even during the toughest parts of the journey."

Jim harbored concerns regarding the coming weekend. The event would be attended by junior high and high school students—not his preferred audience. Working with junior high youth with their uncontrollable prepubescent energy made him uneasy. They would fidget in their seats—an outward sign of their inner distraction. Their lack of attention frustrated him because they would miss both his music and his message, and he didn't know which part of that upset him more. High school kids were a bit easier, but Jim preferred the maturity present in college-aged and young adult audiences because they had made a conscious decision to attend, making his work easier, more rewarding, and productive.

By the time he was headed toward Columbus on March 11, 1983, Jim had more work than he could handle. This would be the last of the five Ohio towns on the current thirteen-day Celebration Shop itinerary, and the extended time away from home was making this trip feel more like a chore than usual. The high demand for his services instilled in him a sense of pride that he had proven his skeptical seminary professors wrong. At the same time, he wondered if he had overbooked his one-man show.

On Friday afternoon, the temperature hovered around freezing as Jim arrived at North Broadway, an old established church near the Ohio State University campus. The agenda for the weekend included a lock-in that night, a full day program and evening concert on Saturday, and the concluding Sunday morning worship service. Jim was beginning to feel like he was running an endless marathon in short intervals but remained determined to find the energy to make the program a dynamic learning experience for those attending. After all, he considered, one never knows how or when God will act in people's lives. This kind of faith kept him going.

Pastor Frank had promised his kids would engage in experience-based teaching and participate in demanding scenarios for them to discuss. Jim's program, weaving together story and song in a unique and engaging fashion, connected with them immediately. They leaned forward in their seats as Jim delivered his modern parables of fictional characters with real-life meaning. They enthusiastically participated in the songs he used to reinforce those messages. According to Pastor Frank, "I remember the feeling of celebration in the worship. Here was a guy who was deeply trained as a minister who had a sensitivity for teens. I remember a feeling of thanksgiving from the parents because they got a glimpse into the level of quality individuals we were bringing to their children."

At a break on Saturday afternoon, Jim chatted with a few of the parents, including Tom and Judy Skinner, who were members of North Broadway. Pastor Frank had asked them to be Jim's hosts for the weekend. As Jim sat with them the night before, he learned that the Skinners had lost their young son Greg to leukemia five years earlier. They shared with him how unprepared they were for Greg's death despite his lengthy illness. As a parent, Jim found the pain and loss that the Skinners had suffered difficult to imagine.

Judy explained that as part of her grieving process she volunteered at the same hospital where her son had died. She described how it saddened her to see children who received few if any visitors. But in her work there she had also witnessed the positive impact when individuals sensitive to the needs of the children did appear.

On Saturday afternoon, after experiencing the first morning of the program, Judy made an inspired connection between capability and opportunity. "Jim, your music is so good, and we see a lot of children at the hospital who don't get a lot of company," she said. "We know the person who heads the volunteer program there. If we can get you in tomorrow afternoon, will you go there to sing for the kids?"

Jim knew agreeing to their request seemed the proper thing to do since the Skinners had been kind enough to provide lodging for the weekend. But a hospital visit would take up most of

Sunday afternoon, the only open time when he could relax or take a needed nap. But deep inside, he recognized that, while this was a plausible reason for his reluctance, it was not the real one. "I had a descending scale of enjoyment from college down to high school and then junior high audiences. I had never even sung for very young children, much less for those who were hospitalized," Jim said. Unable to find a graceful reason to refuse the invitation, Jim consented.

*****

Judy Skinner succeeded in scheduling the appearance, and on Sunday afternoon Jim found himself staring at a forest of IV poles in that fifthfloor hospital waiting area. He faced these very young, severely ill children, their family members, and hospital staff—an audience for which he possessed little material. While he stored an impressive library of adult songs in his musical memory from years of performing, nothing struck him as appropriate for these kids. Raffi's popular song "Apples and Bananas" and Peter, Paul and Mary's hit "Puff the Magic Dragon" were the only children's songs that came to mind. Each time a song entered his conscious mind, the critical side of his brain argued against it. He checked the tuning of his twelve-string guitar to buy more time.

At just that moment, the performing instinct developed through his years on the road kicked in. Experience taught Jim that directionless silence was his worst enemy because it resulted in losing control of the audience and the situation. It was best to pursue an initial course of action and adjust based on audience reaction. Jim launched into the next song that entered his mind. (To this day, he does not recall what that song may have been.)

Early into the number, he spotted a more menacing problem. Nurses had organized the children facing the three elevator doors that opened onto the floor. As soon as he started his first song, the elevator door directly behind him opened, forcing him to slide over to the next one. A couple of moments later, that door opened, carrying visitors who wondered why a tall gentleman and his guitar were blocking their exit. "I couldn't ask everyone to move, so I stood in front of the elevators and started playing." For the next twenty-five minutes, Jim engaged in a game of musical elevators while delivering a program that included songs and smiles, with an occasional wink thrown in for good measure.

"He sang songs that took them out of that place," recalled Pastor Frank, who was in attendance. "Those children were with him, but I am sure they were not with him in that hospital. They were with him on a hillside somewhere. Or they were with him in a park, transported out of their immediate challenging circumstances. He helped release them from their troubles and from their pain and took them to a happy and gracefilled place."

Twenty minutes later, the concert was over, and the crowd offered a polite round of applause. Deflecting their appreciation, Jim thanked them for being a great audience, shook a few hands, and signed a couple of casts. He heaved a sigh of relief, thinking to himself the event had worked out better than expected.

Out of the corner of his eye Jim noticed a nurse hustling in his direction. Still perhaps ten feet away, she called out to him with a sense of urgency in her voice. "Oh please, please. There is this one little boy. He and his mom are in their room and they can't come out. Could you please come and do a song for them?"

Jim sagged. *My God, I thought I was done with this and here I go again.* But much like his response to the Skinners' request the day before, Jim accepted the nurse's invitation while disguising his real sentiment.

The nurse escorted him to a room at the end of a long hall, entered, and signaled for him to follow. Inside, she spoke to a mother with a child in her lap, "This is Jim. He plays guitar and sings. He is going to make you feel better." She spun around and rushed out the door, leaving Jim alone with mother and child, clueless on how to deliver on her bold promise. "I felt completely inadequate."

Jim studied the mother's face. Red circles and dark bags hung beneath both eyes. He could tell she had been crying . . . crying a lot from dealing with her young son's illness. An unfolded blanket and pillow on the daybed offered evidence that she had slept in his room the past few nights. The lines on her face composed a story of determination to be at her son's side and provide whatever comfort she could. It pained Jim to witness the physical signs of the emotional toll the vigil had imposed upon her. "She was a wreck."

Jim looked at the little boy. His frail body made it difficult to determine his exact age, but Jim guessed it to be four or five. The boy's sunken eyes resembled those of an elderly man trapped in a child's body. Although the sight troubled Jim, he found it difficult to take his eyes off him. It was like driving past an accident on the highway—the voice inside that tells you it is impolite to stare loses out to a curiosity that compels you to slow down and look.

"Thank you for letting me come and sing," Jim said, attempting to deflate the internal tension he felt building. For the second time in his life, only a short while after the first, the expectation that he would be providing music added to his anxiety. "I was hoping Scotty from Star Trek would just beam me up and get me out of there," he said later.

Jim played the first song that came to mind—this time the one about "that rascal Puff." When the song was over, both mother and child sat in stone-faced silence. "They looked at me and I looked at them. I didn't know how to exit gracefully, so I just started playing another song."

In the middle of this second song, the little boy lifted his head a bit higher and made eye contact with Jim. Like a drooping flower refreshed by a summer rain, this child who had appeared almost lifeless moments before sat more erect. A slight lift at the corners of his mouth signaled a new spirit emerging.

It was all the encouragement Jim needed to keep playing and singing, hoping to coax a fuller and more undeniable smile. Without missing a beat, he continued into a third song. The boy found the strength to move his small hands, clapping out of sync with Jim's strumming, but his lack of rhythm mattered little because a huge grin flashed across his face. "It lit up the room," Jim said, "and it took the mother by surprise." She looked down and around at her son whom she cradled in her lap as tears began streaming down her face. "It was a torrent," recalled Jim. "She wasn't wailing or anything. They were quiet tears. But it got me going. I was crying and singing at the same time. All the while, the little boy was having a great time.

"This was a joyous moment. It completely took me to another place. I had never experienced any moment more powerful than the twenty or thirty magical seconds that happened at the end of that third song. When I was done, there was no more awkwardness. We could talk."

"Thank you so much. This was wonderful," the mother said. Her child, seated on her lap, was still smiling.

"You are welcome."

They chatted for a few more minutes before Jim, sensing the brief concert had sapped their limited energy, felt it time to excuse himself. When he turned to leave, the mother placed her child on his bed and escorted Jim to the door. As they shook hands, she looked Jim in the eyes. Her voice cracking, she said, "I can't tell you how important this was for us because I don't think we're going to be able to take Toby [not his real name] home from the hospital this time. I think we are going to lose him. He hasn't clapped his hands to music since I can remember. He hasn't smiled like that in weeks. This was a priceless gift that you have given us today. Thank you. Thank you!"

Only silence remained in the common area when Jim returned, everyone from the earlier audience having retired to their rooms. In the quietness of that space, Jim struggled to make sense out of what had just transpired, running the last scene over and over through his mind. He entered the room of this mother and child carrying a bad attitude. He knew no material appropriate for the situation. He found the experience awkward and considered himself inadequate. Yet somehow, despite everything stacked against it, the gift of music Jim provided that day lifted a gravely ill child out of his pain and hopelessness and brought him back to life, if only for a few moments. His music had produced a resurrection experience.

"When I walked out of Toby's room, I just thought this might be where I belong. I love singing. People seem to enjoy my doing it. And the need is so great that even though I wasn't prepared to meet it, somehow, by God's grace, I met a little bit of this family's need in spite of my lack of preparedness and my attitude."

As a seminary student, Jim had read works by American theologian Frederick Buechner, who wrote, "The place God calls you to is the place where your deep gladness and the world's deep hunger meet." On that dreary March afternoon in a cold and lonely hospital room in Columbus, Ohio, Jim Newton arrived at a personal understanding of what those words meant. Sharing three songs with a terminally ill child and his mother, Jim had come face-to-face with his life's calling. Jim thought to himself, *This feels like a door I need to walk through to see what happens.*

It would be three years before Jim sang to another child in a hospital.

THE MISSION

CHAPTER TWO

A New Direction

On the flight from Columbus back home to Dallas, Jim pondered his experience singing for Toby and his mother. Was this truly the direction toward which he had been called to serve, or simply another itch that seemed to visit him every few years and move him toward a different path?

Any self-doubts were offset by the emotional energy he felt during his hospital-room visit. The scene kept looping through his mind like an earworm (a song that gets stuck in one's mind that's nearly impossible to shake loose)—the mental picture of Toby clapping out of rhythm, his smile contrasted with the mother's tears, and the transformation from the first few awkward moments to the sense of connection made possible through music. "I remember being full of excitement about this new direction," said Jim. "I could still do music but find a deeper meaning than I received singing songs for healthy youth and young adults."

Jim shared the story with the Celebration Shop board of directors at their next meeting a couple of weeks later, telling them he wanted to pursue this new ministry. The board responded with enthusiasm, telling him to give it a try: "It sounds great. We won't hold you back for a minute."

What *would* hold Jim back were the numerous challenges involved in recasting Celebration Shop into a ministry conducted in hospitals instead of churches and college campuses. There were personal risks to be considered. His current work was thriving, with engagements booked well into the next year. He had established a solid reputation within the church community, evidenced by positive testimonials from Christian clergy and educators alike.

His ministry in song, his personal leadership, and his grasp of the gospel are outstanding.
—United Methodist Church bishop

His leadership provided a sensitive blend of solid theology, good humor, and excellent music, much of which is original.
—Youth minister

More daunting was the matter of funding. Through his Celebration Shop work with youth and young adults, Jim was paid through honoraria from organizations eager to experience his spiritual enrichment program. As one member of his board pointed out, "You know you can't get paid for this, Jim. The hospitals won't pay, and the families shouldn't have to."

While Jim enjoyed the support of many who knew him and his work at Celebration Shop, he soon discovered that his desire to serve the sick instead of the healthy represented a disconnect for some who had supported him in the past. Jim recalls one person saying, "I am not going to give money to Celebration Shop just so Jim Newton can have a salary." According to Jim, "The problem was this new direction started as something I wanted to do, not a need identified by others who got together hoping to support a musician to go into hospitals and offer songs."

One of the more unexpected issues Jim faced was his lack of a repertoire appropriate for children, particularly those in the hospital. He had struggled to find the right songs to sing during his visit to the children's hospital in Columbus. Jim was convinced the songs he would sing there needed to be positive and helpful, but he wondered what that would look like or where he could go for guidance.

Jim thought the pastoral care office would be a good place to start. Hospital chaplains attend to the spiritual and emotional needs of patients and their families, and during seminary Jim had spent his requisite threemonth clinical pastoral education assignment at Parkland Hospital in Dallas. But Parkland treated adults, not children, so a chaplain told Jim to check with the Child Life Department in a children's hospital.

Jim called a friend, a hospital administrator at MD Anderson Hospital in Houston, who put him into contact with Kim Hixson, director of the child life program there. Jim shared his single experience singing in the hospital with her. "I would like to sing in hospitals for kids, but I don't know any appropriate material," he said. "I don't know what messages they need to hear. Can you tell me what to do?"

Kim shared how the child life discipline had grown out of research early in the twentieth century that noted the higher incidence of death among infants deprived of contact with humans. Early child life professionals, armed with their understanding of child psychology, found ways to help children during hospital stays when they were away from familiar surroundings, family, and friends.

During their meeting, Kim told Jim about an upcoming national conference of the Association for the Care of Children's Health (ACCH) in Boston, an organization comprising nearly four thousand child life specialists, play therapists, music therapists, and other professionals committed to caring for the health of children in the United States and Canada. "You should come to that. I will introduce you to others."

Jim found these experts to be a vast resource as they shared stories about their mission to "reduce the negative impact of stressful or traumatic life events and situations that affect the development, health, and well-being of children, youth, and their families." They told him how the children find themselves in a foreign setting outside both their experience and comfort zone. The stress that accompanies hospitalization can feel threatening to a child, overwhelming their ability to cope and, therefore, to heal.

During the severe illness of a child, the entire family is affected as routines are disrupted. Decisions once taken for granted are taken away from parents, contributing to an overwhelming sense of loss of control over their lives. Parents can feel their role as gatekeeper has been co-opted by hospital caregivers. The sick child can take on immense guilt by believing he or she may have done something wrong to cause the situation.

Armed with this new perspective, a plan began to take shape in Jim's mind—one that would balance current commitments through Celebration Shop with future possibilities. He would continue his paid engagements providing spiritual enrichment programs for youth and young adults, but during his travels he would use spare time to meet with child life specialists to gain a deeper understanding of his new audience.

Over the next two years, as he traveled throughout the country carrying on his youth and college work through Celebration Shop, Jim paid visits to dozens of hospitals and many child life experts. He saw how they work to make hospitalization as normal an experience as possible through activities and stories that encourage children to use their own cognitive abilities to process their situation and reduce anxiety. "It became very clear that music, with its ability to tap into emotions, could be a useful resource," recalls Jim.

During this nascent stage of the child life discipline, the specialists had few creative resources at their disposal. A book about Curious George going to the hospital after eating a piece of a jigsaw puzzle was typical of what was available at the time. The story follows the protagonist's admission to the hospital, where he receives a visit from the mayor and conducts a puppet show in a playroom full of other children. The book portrays hospitals as a place where patients are celebrities and the worst thing that happens is getting a shot in the arm.

Jim made a similar assessment of available music. He saw how standard children's songs like "Pop Goes the Weasel" or "The Ants Go

Marching" might be playful, but Jim doubted these were what children needed to hear when they faced fear and pain. Songs about counting numbers, the alphabet, and animals were nice, but Jim deemed their messages (if there were any) superficial to the point of being potentially offensive to children and families facing serious health challenges. The limitations of the current music selections convinced Jim something better was needed. He saw no reason why children's music couldn't help counteract the negative emotional impact of illness while also being engaging.

In time, Jim's questions to the child life community became more specific. "I would ask them what kind of messages the kids needed," Jim recalled. "They said kids feel this way, parents feel this way, and siblings like this. They described the supportive messages they need to hear and the process to help them deal with their situation in a productive manner."

With the insight gained from these child life specialists, Jim began to articulate his new mission as a specific project under the Celebration Shop organizational umbrella. In his project proposal, he described how he planned to use music to address a genuine need. Calling it the ". . . For My Children" project, Jim described his intent and desired outcome in this way:

To children who are frightened, our songs will bring comfort. For those who are angry, the music will allow them to ventilate and verbalize feelings. For those who have withdrawn inside themselves, the singing and listening will draw them out into improved relationships with others. This project will help children cope with their tragic situations.

Jim presented his project proposal to anyone who would listen. "It became the vehicle through which I could appeal to potential donors," recalls Jim. "It helped me articulate my message that I would be serving the children in the hospitals who were facing many challenges. It was about the children, not just something I wanted to do."

Jim's visits to hospitals helped him develop a new set of contacts beyond the church leaders he had been working with over the past few years, experts he knew he could trust. During one visit, a child life specialist posed a question that suggested a way for Jim to address the lack of available material. "You are a songwriter, Jim. Why don't you write some stuff?" The suggestion resonated with Jim and moved him to take a bold step toward developing a new genre of music intentionally crafted to deliver the messages severely ill children needed to hear. But Jim also learned there would be boundaries on the songs he could share in the hospital setting. "By the way, you are not going to be able to use God language here," another told him.

But gaining adequate funding remained a barrier. Jim held the strong belief that the music he created must be of the highest quality. He had seen nonprofits fail not because their causes lacked merit but due to how they were presented to their audiences. "I don't want to be like most nonprofits or churches that I know who basically have a great heart and a great message but they don't package it well. It doesn't sound good, it doesn't look good, and therefore it doesn't really have an impact on people."

Jim resolved that the music he produced would be presented in a manner that would demand the attention of children and parents while making his donors proud. "I wanted this to be the highest quality, something that would meet our clientele's needs. I wanted to do something that could compete with Disney or *Sesame Street*. I wanted to have a look and feel and sound that could stand up in the same room with them." A tall order, but Jim considered it critical to being accepted by parents and healthcare workers—the gatekeepers protecting the children's interests.

Striving for the highest possible quality was laudable, but accomplishing that goal with limited resources was proving to be quite another issue. Jim arrived at what he thought might be the perfect solution to knock down in one fell swoop these multiple challenges he faced. "I needed a bigname personality to help raise funds on their reputation, someone from the musical community who could help us to improve the quality of our music. In order to get better at whatever your craft is, you find someone who is successful at what you want to do and try to emulate them. They pull you from your level to theirs."

Jim decided to recruit a big-name partner—someone successful enough to grab the attention of potential donors and talented enough to bring the new brand of children's music he envisioned to an unmatched level of professionalism. He needed someone to help deliver the quality of music he believed his new mission demanded. But who might that be?

CHAPTER THREE

In His Corner

Jim needed to recruit a partner with star power—someone successful enough for potential donors to regard highly and possessing musical credentials to help with song creation and production. He developed his slate of candidates as impressive as it was short. There was John Denver, whom Jim admired for his infectious enthusiasm and original songs that valued the simpler things in life. Paul Simon and James Taylor were considered, but Jim was unable to find an obvious connection between the more adult nature of their work and his focus on children's material.

One name rose to the top. He was someone Jim listened to while in college, marveling at his group's vocal arrangements and his ability to find the note that blended perfectly with the bandmates to complete the chord. He was a serious musician involved in issues of social justice who at the same time displayed a playful side on stage and a comfort level with songs for children. Jim had decided to recruit Noel Stookey, better known as Paul of the iconic folk trio of Peter, Paul and Mary. Recalled Jim, "When I was thinking about who could help make our songs work for kids in the hospital and also be a fundraising aid, his name just popped in my head. It was just a feeling I had." But how to find him? Why would a star ever agree to participate in this fledgling project?

Jim remembered that Gene Cotton in Nashville had once worked with Noel on a children's project. In 1981, Jim and Paul G. Hill had collaborated with Gene on a project for youth funded by the United Methodist Church called *Songs for a New World,* which included recorded songs covering issues of world hunger, poverty, peace, and social justice. Jim decided to give Gene a call.

"Gene, I think Noel might be the producer we need for the music we will be doing at children's hospitals."

"I worked with Noel on a little project for kids. He is a delightful guy and loves doing things for children," said Gene.

"Can you put me in touch with him?" asked Jim.

"He's a busy guy, but you never know. Give it a try."

Gene gave Jim Noel's address and phone number. Jim wrote down the contact information but, unsure how to best approach someone of Noel's stature and fame, he allowed inertia to take over. He worried that just calling him out of the blue, even with Gene Cotton's referral, was not enough to capture Noel's interest. Jim did nothing for weeks. "I figured Noel would just tell me he was too busy," recalled Jim.

Jim also feared he did not know the right thing to say. He envisioned the scene in his head, testing different sound bites—the one or two sentences that would best summarize his new mission. Paralyzed by selfdoubt, he set Noel's contact information aside.

A couple of months later, during a casual telephone conversation with an old friend, Chuck Weatherford, Jim was handed a lead to spur him into action. Chuck and his wife, Pam, were youth and music ministers at the United Methodist Church in Greggton, a small town in East Texas. Jim was scheduled to conduct a Celebration Shop program for them later in the summer, so he called Chuck to discuss the theme and details for the event. At the end of their conversation, Chuck casually said, "Oh, by the way, you might be interested to know that Noel Stookey and his contemporary Christian group the Bodyworks Band are going to do a concert here in May."

Jim couldn't believe his good fortune. He had postponed calling the star, and now Noel was coming his way. "Really?" asked Jim. "He's the guy at the top of my list of producers for our children's hospital album. Can I come and open for him in concert?"

"No, Jim. I don't think that's possible because he has asked that there be no opening act," replied Chuck.

Jim pleaded his case. "There has to be some way for me to get Noel's attention. I just know deep inside that he could be our producer."

Finally, Chuck suggested a compromise. "Our patron's group sponsoring the concert series is hosting a reception afterward. If you can make it here, I think you can play at the reception."

"Thanks, Chuck. I will be there."

*****

On Sunday, May 5, 1985, Jim soaked up every note of the wonderful music Noel and his band played. "It was a great concert supporting a great ministry," recalled Jim. But he kept rehearsing in his mind the pitch he would give to Noel should he get the opportunity to talk to him about his project.

As the concert concluded, Jim raced to the corner of the church fellowship hall, usually reserved for potluck dinners and wedding receptions. Chuck had assigned him a spot in the corner of the room to play his twelvestring guitar and sing, which at first struck Jim as far from ideal. Early into his first song, the advantages associated with the corner position became apparent. Jim held a clear line of sight to everything going on in the hall, including the movements of his target. He liked how it would appear that he was playing for everyone, with no one suspecting he was there for only one person: Noel. The corner position was proving to be the perfect spot from which to launch his subtle plan.

Jim soon discovered another unexpected benefit of his corner position: the acoustics were great. The sound of his voice and guitar projected throughout the large room. While he sang, Noel and the Bodyworks Band members mingled with the crowd, drinking church punch, engaging in small talk, and accepting compliments. No one was paying much attention to either the music or the man in the corner, but every once in a while, Jim noticed Noel gaze in his direction. However, each time Noel appeared ready to move Jim's way, Noel would be interrupted by another well-wisher seeking to greet the star. From where Jim stood, he had captured Noel's interest if not his company.

Toward the end of the reception, as Jim was nearing the end of a song, a moment of freedom arrived and Noel made his way across the room toward the minstrel. Excited, expectant, Jim's heart skipped as Noel approached.

"You really sound good. Do you do this often?" asked Noel.

"No, I just came here tonight for your concert," said Jim. "I thoroughly enjoyed it."

"I know you have probably been frustrated because no one is listening to you," said Noel. "I am sorry that you have had to endure that. You know, I've been there before myself. I've been that lonely guy standing there playing when no one was paying attention."

"Actually, I am only doing this hoping you would come over and talk to me," said Jim.

"Really?" replied Noel, surprised at the directness of the comment from a man he had introduced himself to only a moment earlier.

Jim launched into the elevator speech he had rehearsed in his mind dozens of times. "I know this is an inappropriate time, but now that I have your attention, I want to tell you that I think you might be the producer of our hospitalized children's music project. The only reason I came here tonight was to ask for an hour of your time to discuss it. I will come anywhere to meet with you."

Noel considered the surprising request, but before he could respond, Jim continued. "Seriously, if we meet and you tell me you're not interested, you won't hear from me again. I am not going to bother you. But I would really appreciate the chance to sit down and talk with you."

"Sure. Let's do that," said Noel. "Here's my assistant's phone number. Tell her I agreed to meet with you. She should be able to arrange something in the next few months."

*****

Energized by the door opening before him, Jim started calling the assistant the next day . . . and the next day . . . and the day after that. "I probably called her at least twenty times over the next month or so," recalled Jim. "I knew she was just doing her job, but she kept putting me off."

Jim grew tired of being held in check. Trusting in the sincerity of Noel's offer to meet with him, during one call Jim made his final plea to the assistant. "I want you to know that I am a really nice guy, and I will never be rude to you. But Noel said he would meet with me and I believed what he said. I will never stop calling unless I get a personal note from him saying he does not want to meet with me. I will call you back again tomorrow, OK?"

"All right," she said. "Wait, Jim. Noel is going to be at the Starplex in Dallas with Peter, Paul and Mary at the end of July. Sometimes between the sound check and concert he will meet with people at his hotel if he has enough energy. He doesn't guarantee it. But if you want to give it a try, that might work."

"Perfect," said Jim. "Put me on the list."

"You can just expect him to call you that day if he is willing to meet with you," she said.

Jim woke on July 27, 1985, more optimistic than ever. It had taken more than two years from the time Jim sang to Toby to get here, but it looked like he would have the audience with Noel he had waited so long to get. Leaving nothing to chance, that morning Jim drove to the hotel where the trio would be staying to deliver an envelope addressed to Noel. The note read, "Here is my phone number. Please give me a little of your time if you can. I hope to hear from you, if not on this trip, hopefully sometime later. Jim Newton."

His anxiety rising all morning, Jim walked for miles around his neighborhood to work off his abundant nervous energy, working through the spiel he would share with Noel if they met. Unable to bear the wait, Jim called the hotel early in the afternoon to see if the trio had arrived.

"How can I direct your call?" asked the operator.

"I am checking to see if Noel 'Paul' Stookey of Peter, Paul and Mary has checked in."

"Just a moment. Let me connect you," she said.

"No, wait!" said Jim, trying to communicate he was only calling to check on the status, not expecting his call to go through to the room.

In the middle of the first ring, Noel picked up the call. "Hello." "Noel, I am so sorry to bother you. This is Jim Newton. I know I was supposed to wait for your call, but I wanted to make sure you got in OK and that you received my message."

"Oh, Jim. I am just reading your note. Can you come over at-four fifteen?"

"Yes, sir! Thank you so much. I will be there."

Noel gave Jim his room number. For the next couple of hours, Jim rehearsed in his mind the most important speech he had ever made in his life. He had to get it right.

"Noel, thanks for meeting with me. Let me tell you about our children's project." Jim related the story about how he had played music for Toby and his mother, how he witnessed the power of music, and that he now considered providing music for severely ill children and their caregivers his mission in life. "I really want to make a difference for these kids musically," he said. "Gene Cotton told me that you have a heart for children."

"I love your voice and your integrity. I think you are the perfect person to be our producer," Jim continued. "But before I ask you to consider this request, I have to tell you one thing. I know you are a committed Christian; I have heard you share your testimony. I am totally comfortable with that because I am a United Methodist Church minister and it is central to my life. But if you are going to work with us, you need to know that we can't use religious language in this project because the hospitals won't let us. Besides, I am committed to reaching all children regardless of their faith background. I think that's what God wants us to do."

Noel sat back, considered the invitation and constraint for a moment, and asked, "Well, if we can't say 'God,' can we say 'love'?"

"Yes, we certainly can!" replied Jim with enthusiasm.

"You know, the Scripture says, 'God is love,' and that will be good enough for me," said Noel. "When I first became a born-again Christian, I would take my faith and throw it at everyone around me," he continued. "I watched people turn away from me over and over again because I was just beating them up with it. I finally decided that if I just lived the way God wanted me to live, that maybe when people saw me living that way, in time they would ask me why. I would tell them when they were ready to hear."

Jim and Noel spent an hour together that afternoon. "He was so easy to talk with that he put me at ease. I couldn't believe it," recalled Jim. "He didn't know me but he said yes." Still marveling years later at the series of events that led to his connecting with Noel, Jim describes it as "a gift from God or just dumb luck or fate, depending on your theology."

Noel depicts their initial meeting in similar terms. "If our meeting was truly divinely inspired, then Jim was the perfect messenger because he was humble. He was standing in the corner and, according to him, he knew if he just stood there and played guitar and sang, because of my heart, my upbringing, or what he sensed in me, I would have to come over and introduce myself."

It had been a bold, perhaps even absurd, plan, but Jim now had the big-name partner he needed joining his mission. "I was dreaming big, but I was nuts enough to think I could do it," said Jim, who now had Noel Stookey in his corner. It was time to create a new kind of children's music.

THE MUSIC

CHAPTER FOUR

The "Inside" Story

The small scribble at the bottom of the page grabbed Noel's attention. Paul G. Hill had only jotted it down as a reminder of the metaphor upon which his song would be based: "You can't judge a book by its cover." But the moment Noel noticed the adage, three things critical to the future of Jim's new mission—the genre of therapeutic music he hoped to create, Paul's new song, and the nature of their working relationship with the folk icon—were all about to get better.

Paul met Jim in 1977 while shopping for a church home. Paul had liked Jim's musical leadership of an informal worship service at Cox Chapel at Highland Park United Methodist Church in Dallas so much that he had asked Jim if he needed help. Jim was leery of a walk-up musician wanting to volunteer in church, but he had Paul audition and gave him a part. It was the beginning of a friendship and musical partnership that would still be active almost forty-five years later.

With his degree in music theory and composition from SMU, Paul possessed skills that complemented Jim's folk music background by providing the discipline he sometimes lacked. "He was more of a songwriter than I was and a better one. I asked him to turn his great composition skills into songs for kids," said Jim.

Jim and Paul began to search for messages they might include in their first recording project. The child life experts had convinced Jim about how important it was for the songs to carry messages sensitive to what severely ill children and their families were experiencing.

Standards like "Row, Row, Row Your Boat" were lighthearted but that was not what children needed to hear when they were not feeling very playful. As Paul said, "We wanted the music to have more meaning than singing the ABCs."

A quick scan of children's songbooks revealed that the music was organized by subject, pointing to how unique a message-centered approach would be. Material was traditionally sorted into categories, such as

- Animals ("Old McDonald," "Baa Baa Black Sheep")

- Counting ("The Ants Go Marching")

- Alphabet ("ABC Song")

- Stories ("Mary Had a Little Lamb")

- Playtime ("Skip to My Lou")

- Singing Rounds ("Row, Row, Row Your Boat")

Songs like these have remained popular because they are entertaining and structured in ways that teach basic reading, counting, and musical skills. While a careful listen to some of the standards might reveal positive messages like perseverance ("Itsy Bitsy Spider") and generosity ("Baa Baa Black Sheep") embedded in some of the lyrics, it would be a stretch to say they came anywhere near addressing the emotional needs of severely ill children.

As innocent and as wholesome as traditional children's songs appear to be, when viewed through the eyes of a child, many contain lyric content or depict scenes ranging from insensitive to downright disturbing for even the healthiest of children. Some songs discuss tragic events ("London Bridge") or the killing of animals ("Farmer in the Dell") or the violent use of weapons ("Three Blind Mice").

More troubling was the fact that the messages contained in many popular numbers were inappropriate for use in the hospital setting. Wellknown songs containing images of cradles holding children falling to the ground ("Rock-a-Bye Baby") or children suffering broken bones from falls ("Jack and Jill") and injuries that could not be mended ("Humpty Dumpty").

Newer artists in the 1980s like Tom Chapin, Rosenshonz, and Raffi were writing and recording engaging children's songs with higher production quality. But to Jim's and Paul's ears, most of this work failed to hit the mark for the specific audience they were trying to reach. The unique physical and emotional needs of the hospitalized children demanded a more sensitive approach if the music had any chance of being helpful. They needed messages that encouraged them to persevere, helped them express their feelings, and built their self-esteem.

Jim and Paul began composing original songs that would balance the somewhat incongruent goals of working artistically while remaining sensitive to the situations faced by hospitalized children. Jim described their process and goals in an update to early supporters of his ". . . For My Children" project in this way:

> **Our approach is to get in touch with the children and with those who know them best—parents, family members, hospital staff—and to let them tell us what is needed and helpful. We are creating a new artistic resource, which flows out of the therapeutic need it is addressing. We will do more than merely entertain and help those hurting people pass the time. We will be a vital link to the healing process!**

While his formal training provided a nice balance to Jim's free-flowing folk background, Paul was skeptical at first about the new songwriting direction and audience. "Quite frankly, I was not interested in doing children's music. But I told Jim that if we could make it interesting children's music, I would certainly work with him."

Jim's success recruiting Noel Stookey to act as producer for the recording phase assuaged Paul's concerns. The plan was that Noel would maintain quality control over all aspects of the project, from selecting the material to blessing the final recording mix. Noel said, "I'll come down, and if I like what you are doing, you can call me producer and I will put my name on it." Toward that end, Noel recruited friend and keyboard player Denny Bouchard to contribute his talents during their studio work. The team was getting the professional support from Noel they had envisioned. "He brought musical legitimacy to what we were doing," said Paul.

While Noel and Denny's involvement was a blessing, it also contributed to Jim's growing anxiety about the future. The stakes were now higher. For their partnership to work, Jim and Paul would need to elevate their musical game. Jim told Paul, "If we don't produce, Noel is probably going to drop away from us."

The pressure was heightened by the fact that Jim and Paul were setting sail into uncharted creative territory, attempting to write songs that addressed the specific emotional needs of hospitalized children. It represented a Copernican shift where the songs revolved around the needs of the audience rather than the messages the writer wanted to communicate. They were not sure anyone had ever approached songwriting in this manner, except perhaps those who composed jingles for TV and radio ads. Nor were Jim and Paul confident they were up to the task. According to Paul, "To attempt to speak to someone else's emotional predicament and to do so with integrity is a large order. It was like we were given a prescription from hospital workers and asked to fill it. That, in and of itself, is a different kind of thing than what most songwriters did, where the primary drive was to say something personal and hope it connected with other people." Jim felt much the same. "I never had a child who was chronically or severely ill. I never had a child who died. As a result, I am not equipped to write out of my personal need on those issues," said Jim.

During the early stages of their work, Jim and Paul assumed their songs needed to include a direct connection to the hospital experience. They wrote about situations the children were going through, like chemotherapy, and tried to translate into lyrics what these children's feelings might be. However, including medical references in the songs was stifling the creative process until they received direction from an unexpected source.

In the mid-1980s, Jim and Paul attended a conference of the Association for the Care of Children's Health, a consortium of healthcare professionals and parents committed to family-centered care. At a workshop, they presented their emerging philosophy and approach to therapeutic music. They shared early versions of songs and invited feedback. The room went silent when one woman approached the microphone because few parents attended this conference and those who did attend rarely spoke. Her message was brief and to the point. "I'm the mother of a child with a severe disease. I don't want my daughter to think she is special because she is sick. I want her to feel special because of *who she is*."

Her comment was consistent with a viewpoint articulated by a wellknown physician at MD Anderson in Houston, Dr. Jan van Eys. In his book *The Normally Sick Child*, he suggested that human existence is lived on a continuum that runs from sickness to wellness. While most people think it is abnormal for children to get sick, it is actually "normal" for human beings to alternate between sickness and health. He argued that if we treat childhood sickness as an abnormality, we risk interfering with their emotional, physical, and spiritual development. Therefore, healthcare workers and parents need to not only seek the biological cure for the sick child but also find ways to support their entire well-being.

The mother's comment and Dr. van Eys's philosophy provided a breakthrough for Jim and Paul, liberating them from the need to use clinical terminology. It meant the positive messages they hoped to capture in their songs would be helpful in a broader context. Although the need to hear these messages would be more acute for those hospitalized, they could benefit all children.

*****

In late 1986, Paul was working on a song directed at building the sense of positive self-regard among children. In his composition titled "Inside," Paul wanted to communicate that no matter how a child might feel or look, they were still valued as a human being. "I wanted this to be a song about not putting up walls based on appearances, both in the way we look at others and the way we look at ourselves," said Paul. "My idea came from the old adage 'You can't tell a book by its cover.' That was the song's central concept."

Fearing the saying lacked the incisive edge he was looking for in the song, Paul never considered it for a verse. He looked at various candidates before selecting topics for the first two verses, each a direct translation of the "book" metaphor into another object. The first verse included this line:

You can't tell which pie tastes best if you only eat the crust

The second verse stated,

You can't tell which gift you like best just by looking at the bow

In December 1986, Jim and Paul were scheduled to meet with Noel to share their early work and gain his input. Draft lyrics to the first two verses and the chorus of "Inside" were in place, but no music had been written. While Paul felt the piece was too incomplete, Jim believed showing Noel preliminary work would be an effective way to engage him. In the end, Jim prevailed.

Noel nodded his head when he read Paul's initial draft of "Inside," something he tended to do when encountering something to his liking. "This is an important idea. I would really like to help finish this one," he said. Noel locked in on the song's working metaphor about book covers and contents. Paul had written the phrase down to help him stay focused, but Noel saw it as a key part of the project. "I like that idea. I think I'll write that verse."

In addition to his work on the third verse, Noel made a simple but effective suggestion to set up each verse. Rather than begin by stating the object, like a pie or gift or a library book, Noel added an introductory line that established the song's context and invited the listener into the scene. The revised verses opened with these lines:

Let's say you're at this pie contest
Let's say that you're the judge

Let's say you're at this birthday party
And say you just turned two

Let's say you're at this library

And there's stacks and stacks of books

Paul's responsiveness to Noel's suggestions cemented their developing relationship. According to Noel, "Here were the two of us, at a distance in the early beginning, trying to be as honest as we could about a piece of music. It was one of those things where you say to yourself, *If I can't be myself and say absolutely anything that comes to mind, then is this the kind of involvement I want to continue?* So, from the get-go, I was blunt about where I thought the song should go. Paul's response was like we were brothers, like it was in the family, like it wasn't unusual at all for him to deal with these outrageous suggestions."

Noel suggested the song needed a musical device to break the monotony of three verses similar in structure. Paul wrote a bridge, a short section usually in the middle of a song that contrasts with the verses and choruses:

Children are the very best
Each one a joy and pride
Just how we know, I'll bet you guessed
We took the time to look inside

Instead of ending the bridge with a closed thought, Noel suggested stopping short of the last word to dramatize the song's central message.

We took the time to look . . .

This allowed the listener to imagine the word "inside" before it was sung twice at the start of each line in the chorus for added emphasis:

Inside, inside, that's the most important part Inside,
inside, that's the place you've got to start
Inside, inside, that's where you'll find the heart of the matter

The final version of "Inside" uses three different situations (a pie contest, a birthday party, and a visit to a library) to drive home a singular message that a person's inner self is what matters most. It affirms that everyone is worthy of being valued and loved regardless of race, color, creed, or medical condition.

The team felt so good about "Inside" that Jim, Paul, and Noel decided to record it as soon as possible. In the studio, Noel's personality, experience, and innate ability to create characters kicked into high gear. When Noel took his place before the microphone he asked, "Can I do anything I want here?" Jim encouraged him to do whatever he felt would work. When the tape started running, Noel introduced the song by making the sound effect of a truck noisily backing up to deliver pies. He portrayed distinct characters (a dockworker, a young child, and a librarian) for the three verses. When he was finished, Noel wondered out loud, "Gosh, maybe that was a little bit over the top." Everyone there loved it. It was the kind of ownership and creative license Jim had hoped for when he invited Noel to be musical adviser for the project.

Noel described the finished recording of "Inside" in this way: "There was a kind of playfulness that gives the listener permission to engage in the game of listening. There was participation and interaction, making the song into a drama or into a little play in miniature. It becomes part of the experience so listeners don't get tired of the music."

The recording captured the blend of sentiment and style Jim and Paul had in mind when they started their songwriting process. "Inside" became an engaging treatment of an important message, affirming the inherent goodness in all of us while holding a special place for the little ones who "are the very best."

*****

Noel liked "Inside" so much he convinced bandmates Peter Yarrow and Mary Travers to include it on a children's album they made together a couple of years later. On the trio's version recorded before a live audience of children and their families at Brooklyn's Majestic Theater in November 1992, each member took lead vocals on a verse. Noel sang the verse he wrote with an air of sophistication in his voice that bordered on haughty. While he bellowed about "stacks upon stacks of books," his singing mates "shushed" him to be quiet. "It's a library, Noel," whispered Peter. The admonition worked for only a few lines until Noel reverted back to his animated state and loud voice. It was performed in classic Stookey style, bringing both character and song to life in an engaging and memorable manner.

Upon learning that "Inside" would be included on the album, Paul was delighted. *How cool is this?"* he thought. Better yet, *Peter, Paul and Mommy, Too* was nominated for the Grammy Award in the Best Musical Album for Children category in 1994, losing out to the soundtrack for the movie hit *Aladdin*.

The sense of accomplishment that came with having his song recorded was surpassed a couple of years later when Paul attended a Peter, Paul and Mary concert at the Dallas Starplex with his brother, sister-in-law, and Jim. After performing "Inside," Noel asked Paul to stand. In front of thousands of fans, he acknowledged Paul for his work on the piece. According to Paul, "When that recognition came, something that I had craved for so long, I just felt gratitude to Noel, to the trio, and to the circumstances of my life. It was just pure affirmation."

Paul has remained proud of the work. "I thought it spoke well to the issue of self-esteem, reminding children who found themselves limited by their illness that the important thing was their inner self. Their true worth was not affected by their health challenges. This concept also spoke very concretely about the issue of diversity and not judging others by their appearance or other surface traits, without talking down to children."

According to Paul, Noel jokingly referred to "Inside" as "that song I stole from you." Although the song originated from Paul's imaginative concept and he wrote most of the lyrics and all the music, they equally share rights. "Somehow I don't feel I've been robbed," said Paul. What he received in return was a strong working relationship with an ally Paul and Jim needed to succeed.

Noel entered this relationship expecting his involvement would be limited but found collaboration with Jim and Paul easy and rewarding. Noel witnessed their desire to produce quality music in support of a cause that resonated with him. "That first song sucked him in," said

Jim. "He respected our various talents and commitment. Plus, he got more in touch with the needs of the kids and felt he could make a difference. Noel likes making a difference."

"Inside" was more than a nice song. It provided Jim and Paul confidence they could create more music that expressed targeted messages in an engaging fashion. It defined the standard for what meaningful therapeutic music for children needed to be: songs that contained a playfulness while delivering serious messages for consideration and reflection.

Their productive collaboration on "Inside" forged a new partnership upon which Jim, Paul, and Noel could build. According to Noel, "The first appreciation of what they were up to was when Paul shared with me his early lyric rendering. The two of us were able to speak about how many different ways the inside of a person could be revealed and what those metaphors might be. So, when Paul and I would throw these ideas back and forth about birthday parties and opening presents and discovering what's inside, or a library and opening up a book, those kind of parables and images resonated with both of us. We felt like we were both on the same track."

"Inside" may have been the first original song the team recorded, but it accomplished more than that. Paul felt validated, Noel was engaged, and Jim was energized. "We need more songs like that one," he said with a smile.

CHAPTER FIVE

Songs That Matter

"Inside" may have gained some unexpected notoriety, but it represented something far more important. It demonstrated that songs containing helpful messages could also be entertaining. Over the subsequent forty years, the team has built a library of over 140 songs, plus Spanish-language versions of nearly a third of them. Most are original compositions, but many are songs from other artists that the team and their panel of experts deemed fit their criteria.

Their recordings have captured numerous awards, such as three Parents' Choice Awards, the Family Channel Seal of Quality, recognition as an American Library Association Notable Children's Recording, and a Parent's Guide Children's Media Award, among many others. The recognition they received was an outcome, not the goal of their work. "I saw the awards as a way to support our core message with donors," said Jim. "It was an affirmation that songs containing positive messages produced at the highest possible quality can make a difference."

By the late 1980s, Jim and Paul had defined the wide array of messages they sought to deliver in their genre of therapeutic music for children. Some were directed at individual needs, others toward both caregivers and patients. Some addressed emotions that needed to be offset by music, while others represented areas where positive reinforcement would be helpful.

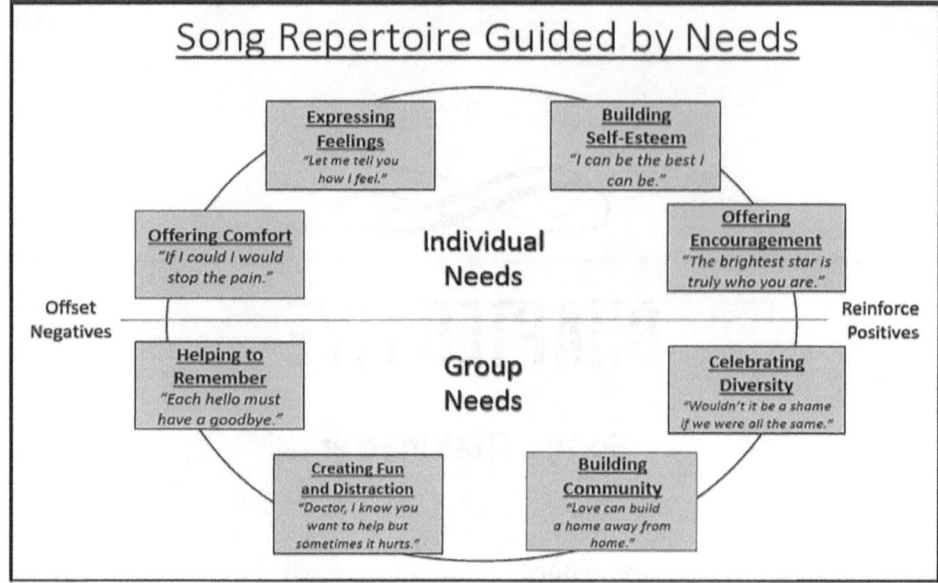

It would be a gross oversimplification to suggest that any song addresses only a single emotional need. A song that helps a child express his or her feelings can also build self-esteem, and one that offers comfort might also serve as a distraction or provide meaning during a time of mourning. The potential combinations are almost endless. But for most songs in the repertoire, a clear intent regarding the desired message each song would communicate guided the composition from original idea to final production.

The following sections describe the backstories to some of the most popular songs in the new KidLinks genre of therapeutic music, organized around eight critical message areas. (Note: Many of the songs covered here were created and recorded under the aegis of three different organizations, but for simplicity the current KidLinks name is used throughout.) These stories are intended to bring the songs and the songwriting process to life, demonstrate the lengths the team went through to create music that matters to its audience, and share stories of how these songs have positively impacted listeners.

"THE FROG SONG" (EXPRESSING FEELINGS)

One consistent message from the interviews with child life specialists was the need for children to connect with and express their feelings. They described how children who are hospitalized may find it difficult to verbalize their fears, and these pent-up emotions can inhibit the healing process.

While Paul focused his writing energy on the need to build self-esteem, Jim took the lead on the area of feeling expression. Jim sensed that music possessed the inherent ability to elicit and express emotions that could help children battle through tough times. Further, this need was also shared by parents and staff because blocking their own emotions might hinder their ability to share their love and caring with the children. "Music is a natural expresser, and we all need that," said Jim.

Jim started "The Frog Song," and Noel helped finish it. To make the song's message accessible to young children, Jim used the time-tested tactics of repetition and the use of animals to engage his audience. According to Jim, "'The Frog Song' was a fun way to talk about the fact that we all have feelings. Kids will connect with simple, silly songs. They sort of 'make friends' with a song. They like repetition so much that they will sing it over and over again."

"The Frog Song" uses animals and insects to engage the audience. It also uses a call-and-response format where an initial phrase sung by the leader prompts an audience answer:

Call: **I'm a little frog**
Response: **I'm a little frog**
Call: **Sittin' on a log**
Response: **Sittin' on a log**
Let me tell you how I feel

Once the characters have been introduced, the song names a range of emotions that might need to be expressed: gladness, sadness, silliness, seriousness, friendliness, loneliness, and everything in between:

Call: **Sometimes I feel glad**
Response: **Sometimes I feel glad**
Call: **Sometimes I feel sad**
Response: **Sometimes I feel sad**
Sometimes I don't feel at all

The underlying principle is that feelings are neither good, bad, nor indifferent. They are just feelings, and it is healthy for children to express them in appropriate ways. "Anything we can do to help them get in touch with their feelings is good," said Jim.

On the last verse, listeners are invited to fill in the blanks and in a unified voice express their feelings. Because they have been singing the response to each line since the start of the song, vocalizing personal emotions seems natural at this point:

Sometimes I feel_____.

Sometimes I feel_____.

Sometimes I just feel_____.

"I wanted to give them a 'process song' that encouraged them to get in touch with and communicate their feelings," said Jim. "You can ask kids how they feel, but they are not going to tell you. They might not even understand the question. But if you sing a silly song, they might blurt out, 'I'm mad' or 'I'm happy' or 'I'm sad.' A song gives them permission and a safe place to let out their feelings."

"The Frog Song" took center stage in a national broadcast of the CBS news program *Street Stories,* hosted by newsman Ed Bradley. Aired in April 1993, the segment told the story of an eleven-year-old girl who had contracted the AIDS virus through "no identifiable reason" (the title for this episode). No one knew how or where she had been exposed to the disease. As they followed her to the hospital for her regular treatment, the reporter said, "She learned a song there that helps her feel better."

The little girl began to sing, "I'm a little frog, sittin' on a log. Let me tell you how I feel."

Jim didn't recognize the little girl, although it was possible that she had attended one of the summer camps he had visited or he had sung it with her in the hospital. Regardless, the song provided a vehicle through which she chose to express herself. The little girl went on to discuss a topic even adults can find difficult, telling the correspondent and a national audience, "Dying doesn't scare me. I know I'm going to die soon. But I'm not afraid. You shouldn't be afraid because after you die there is a light that guides you to heaven, and if you get lost, an angel will help you."

That is exactly how Jim hoped "The Frog Song" would work. "I don't know how to explain it. There is probably some brain research that supports it from a scientific perspective, but I know from experience that there is a direct and powerful connection between organized tones (which we call music) and the human feelings we have. Music is a natural highway for our feelings. It can stimulate us. It can relax us. It can certainly move us and our feelings. Our songs help kids connect with their feelings because music is a direct pathway to our emotions. The central message may not always be self-expression, but the connection to feelings is there in all of them."

"I CAN BE THE BEST I CAN BE" (BUILDING SELF-ESTEEM)

Strengthening the sense of self-worth for young children going through hospitalization was an obvious need coming out of Jim's early interviews with experts. They described how illness adversely impacts children's abilities to cope with their diseases and the clinical environments in which they find themselves. Children with low self-esteem may interpret temporary problems to be more substantial than is actually the case. Or children may believe they had something to do with bringing the disease upon themselves and their families, and a lower sense of self-worth can develop.

It was no accident that Paul and Noel's composition "Inside" was among the first original songs recorded by the team because it made a global statement regarding the worth of all children. But to help children embrace the message that they were valued despite their illnesses, Paul believed a first-person treatment of this theme would be effective. Out of this insight emerged the song with a title that sums up its message: "I Can Be the Best I Can Be." This song translated the global message underlying "Inside" into a personal one.

Written in first person, Paul used repetition of the title phrase accompanied by an engaging singsong melody, easy for first-time listeners to learn. Each of the song's two verses is loaded with images designed to capture the attention of the youngest of listeners:

> **I can't stand on a distant planet**
> **I can't stand on my sister Janet**
> **I can't stand on a rhino's snout**
> **I can't stand brussels sprouts**
> **I can't drive a circus train**
> **And I can't drive a big jet airplane**
> **I can't drive my dad to work**
> **But sometimes I drive Mom berserk**

The chorus does all the heavy lifting for the song, repeating its central message to make it inescapable:

> **But I can be the best I can be**
> **I can be the best I can be**
> **Take a look at me and you'll see**
> **I can be the best I can be**
> **I can do the best I can do**
> **I can do the best I can do**
> **And I'm gonna bet you can, too**
> **You can do the best you can do**

The chorus is repeated three times, once following each verse plus the bridge. By the end of the song, the phrases of encouragement about being "the best I can be" and doing "the best I can do" are repeated eighteen times, making it impossible to miss the song's core theme. The silliness of each verse serves as the appetizer; the chorus is the abundant main course.

As is the case for most songs, the bridge sums up the song's core message:

> **If there are things that I can't do**
> **If there are things that I can't be**
> **When I try my very best**
> **I'm still the best at being me**

Jim has always found something deeper in that last line. "Most people go through life measuring who they are by what they can or can't do. When you move from centering on acting as a human 'doing' to seeing yourself as a human 'being,' it's an incredibly freeing experience."

Paul describes the origins and intent of the song in this manner: "As far back as I can remember, we began asking what messages children needed to hear. One of the discussions that impacted me was how important it is to sense one's self-worth by just being who we are. It is very important for children not to feel limited by their medical circumstances or bodily challenges. So that was the idea—that *just being me* was equal to being *my best me*."

Jim goes even further, suggesting that the principle of "unconditional caring and love" underlies original compositions like "Inside" and "I Can Be the Best I Can Be" because they speak to the inherent value of all individuals regardless of appearance, illness, race, gender, or beliefs. "Because music has the inherent ability to touch hearts, when it is offered in the true spirit of unconditional love it can be a significant source of healing," said Jim.

In 1999, KidLinks was recognized with the Children's Hospice International Elisabeth Kübler-Ross Award for Outstanding Contribution. The award recognizes "an individual who made a significant difference in the field of hospice-type care for children with life-threatening conditions."

Dr. Kübler-Ross was best known for defining the five stages of grief, and Jim had read all of her books while in seminary. "When we received that award in her name, I was blown away because I valued her work so much," he said.

A few years later, Jim and Paul attended a daylong celebration of Dr. Kübler-Ross's life and work sponsored by a hospice group in Maine. At the beginning of the program, Jim recalled the guest of honor was lifted up on the stage because she was confined to a wheelchair after suffering several small strokes. Friends and colleagues read poems, offered testimonials, and showed a video paying tribute to her.

According to Jim, event sponsors had told attendees not to expect her to talk that day, given her physical condition. But at the end of the program, the master of ceremonies asked Dr. Kübler-Ross if there was anything she wanted to say to the group. She held out her hand for the microphone and said, "I am going to sum up for you in one sentence what I learned in all my years of studying death and dying." After a long pause, she continued, "People who have experienced unconditional love during their life will die in peace, and those who haven't will not." She then handed the microphone back to the moderator.

That was it—a single sentence that left a lasting impression on Jim. "I think it is true," he said. "We somehow die inside if we don't have someone who will accept us for who we are. We all need to be loved completely no matter what. That kind of love heals all wounds."

According to Jim, "I Can Be the Best I Can Be' is the signature KidLinks song. It is the most central to the heart of our philosophy. If I had to pick only one song to sing, this would be it."

"SHINE SO BRIGHT" (OFFERING ENCOURAGEMENT)

Children suffering from severe or chronic illnesses find themselves on lengthy journeys where they encounter unfamiliar symptoms, treatments, and surroundings. They may be unable to process what is happening in a way that helps them sustain their emotional energy over the long haul. Jim and Paul recognized that songs offering support and encouragement in the face of such challenges needed to be an important part of their repertoire.

Nowhere were the long-term challenges that accompany fighting a disease more obvious than in the pediatric cancer camps that Jim began serving in 1985. For the next five years, Jim spent more than twice as many service days playing music at camps (129) than he did in hospitals (55). Facilities with names like Camp UKANDU and Camp Kemo provided Jim the chance to interact with the children who were still battling or had beaten their illnesses. Children with missing limbs and bald heads may not be able to handle standard summer camp routines and facilities. Some may have trouble getting into showers or toilet facilities found at other camps. However, these special-needs camps are designed with the physical requirements of the pediatric cancer patient in mind.

The children Jim met at these camps provided an unvarnished perspective on issues the child life specialists had described, making them more real and human. He heard about their long journeys, leading him to see the need for songs that reframed negative circumstances into a positive mindset.

Jim quickly realized that summer camps offered both a source of inspiration and the perfect venues for developing and testing new material. Singing with the children at least three times a day for an entire week demanded an expanded repertoire to prevent the sessions from becoming too repetitive and boring. Through multiple exposures of an emerging song in front of the same audience, Jim was able to identify which ones merited further work versus those that needed to be dropped.

Everyone from campers to doctors, nurses, and staff understood the challenges these children were facing. These kids didn't have to tell others their stories to feel that they belonged. At cancer camp, children who were battling this disease discovered that they were not alone. The experience made the abnormal normal, which was hugely important for them. In fact, many of the counselors had attended years earlier as campers and returned to guide others through a meaningful camp experience.

If the magic of cancer camp was helping these children realize they were not alone in their illness, the music there made this sense of community real. Campers and counselors may be scattered in all directions with activities throughout the day, but music represented something everyone could do together. Three music sessions of thirty minutes each day provided the children a chance to learn the KidLinks tunes and access the deeper messages behind the lyrics. Singing with others and hearing their collective voices bounce powerfully off the walls knock down barriers while creating an inescapable and powerful sense of community. Janet Johnson, the first director of Camp Star Trails, said, "Music is the heart of our camp."

Through experience, Jim learned that at cancer camp music was a powerful force because, for these children, emotions easily rise to the surface yet are deeper at the same time. He described it this way:

"Kids who have been or are at risk are more in touch with their feelings because they have had to be. Things connect with them at a deeper level. So when they are in an accepting and safe environment and a song comes along they enjoy, they feel free to respond with their whole heart and soul."

One inspirational tradition at Camp Star Trails has been the candle lighting ceremony held on the last night. Earlier that day, each child is asked to write down his or her favorite memory of the week and express a wish for the future. The paper holding that wish is tied to the wishes of fellow cabinmates to symbolize the friendships that developed during the week. These bundles of wishes become the focal point of the closing ceremony.

As darkness settles over the grounds, campers walk to the nearby lake. Glow necklaces worn by each camper add a magical touch to the solemn occasion. As the campers take their seats on benches facing the roaring bonfire next to the lake, Jim stands to the side singing comforting melodies written for the occasion. One by one, the cabins come forward to share their wishes aloud. Trust that has developed during their week together makes this a safe place to express their greatest hopes and fears. The chain of wishes is then tossed into the flames while a member of the cabin lights a candle placed on a large wooden star attached to an inner tube that lies flat on a table. After the last candle is lit, the wooden star is carried to the lake, where it floats away from the shore toward the distant horizon.

That scenic moment is Jim's cue to begin singing "Shine So Bright," his original song of encouragement dedicated to these young campers who represent metaphorical stars who brighten our daily lives:

I can see your faces in the morning when you rise
I can see you when you're busy sleeping
And throughout the day you give your best in every way
The light-shine of your stars fills up my sky

The bridge captures a realistic portrayal of the journeys these children continue to go through, affirming that they will always be stars despite setbacks and challenges they may encounter:

Every now and then a star will go behind a cloud
We all need a little rest, a chance to rain
But before you know it there it is, a'sparkling once again
For within the darkness glows the brightest star
And the brightest star is truly who you are

By the time Jim reaches the closing chorus, the wooden star carrying the precious cargo of candles representing wishes for the future is glowing off in the distance. Total darkness has fallen over Camp Star Trails as Jim sings the positive charge of encouragement expressed in the final chorus:

Shine so bright, livin' off the light
Shine so bright, I see you sparkle
Shine so bright, something must be right
Shine forever toward the dawn

"Shine So Bright" expresses the enduring impression that cancer camps had on Jim. He marveled at how these children threw their weak bodies but strong spirits into camp activities, including his music. He saw that they did not act like victims waiting for a miracle to arrive. Cancer could not be something to merely wish away because the disease was no longer something that happened to them; it was part of who they were: beautiful children who, despite their illnesses—or perhaps because of them—represented stars destined to "shine forever toward the dawn."

"WOULDN'T IT" (CELEBRATING DIVERSITY)

One of the overarching goals of child life specialists is to help children and their families cope with the challenges of hospitalization. Children in the hospital who have lost their hair or strength may begin to see themselves as "not normal" and perhaps inferior to their peers. Research has shown that a factor most strongly associated with a successful emotional outcome following serious illness is the extent to which a child is able to reappraise his or her situation and extract something positive from the experience.

Jim and Paul believed that music could facilitate a positive adjustment to the hospital environment by asserting the inherent value of each individual regardless of the child's disease, background, or appearance. One KidLinks song that came directly out of this intent was "Wouldn't It" written by Paul. "We listed a lot of subjects we wanted to address through our music, and 'diversity' was at the top of the list," Paul explained. "I wanted to address that by saying that it is not only OK that we are diverse but that it is exciting that we are so diverse."

Paul's playful lyrics in "Wouldn't It" uses easy-to-understand metaphors to encourage children to view our differences in a more positive and profound way. Each verse poses a variation on a simple theme, suggesting how unfortunate it would be if all the colors, the ice cream flavors, or the seasons of the year were the same. Take, for example, the first verse:

Blue's the color I like best
Except, of course, for all the rest
Orange, yellow, red, and green
And all the others in between

The final two lines of each verse affirm the song's core message that it is only through our differences that life becomes interesting:

Wouldn't it be a shame if all the [colors] [flavors] [seasons]
were the same
It wouldn't be very fun if there were only one

The song's final verse extends the metaphor beyond objects to include relationships with others, cementing the message about inclusiveness and acceptance:

You're the friend that I like best Except, of course, for all
the rest And when all is said and done
We could be friends with everyone

But on the final chorus, Paul summarized the song's core message and inserted two additional words, sung after a short pause, intended to leave listeners with something to consider:

Wouldn't it be a shame if we were all the same. Wouldn't it?

The context in which children experience many KidLinks songs like "Wouldn't It" enhances the positive effect. When played as part of a group sing-along in hospital playrooms or at summer camps, the music is particularly effective at supporting children who feel they might be somehow less than others.

According to Jim, "One of the things we want children to know is that we accept them with all their differences—that we should embrace our differences rather than judge them because our differences enrich us, not diminish us." Paul's composition "Wouldn't It" does just that.

"FRIENDS OF THE FAMILY" (BUILDING COMMUNITY)

When children enter the hospital, they encounter dozens of new faces in the first few hours. Forced to say goodbye to their pets, friends, and familiar surroundings, children enter a foreign world where customary routines are replaced by policies and procedures to which they are unaccustomed.

New and meaningful relationships are regularly established in this context. People from vastly different backgrounds become like neighbors who look after one another. "When we first started singing in the hospitals, we were struck by the sense of community that was built between child patients and their siblings, from family to family, and between family and staff," said Jim. "It just blew us away."

"Friends of the Family" was one of the first songs that Jim, Paul, and Noel wrote because it celebrated the fundamentally human need to feel the support of a larger community. The opening lines of the tune capture what it is like to feel like a stranger entering an unfamiliar world:

Ever been some place so strange and new
Didn't know one face, didn't know just what to do

Having established the emotional context, the lyrics offer comfort by asserting that the writer can empathize with their situation:

I've been there too

Felt just like you

"We noticed that these families were building friends for a lifetime at the hospital," recalled Jim. "That was the concept we built the song out of, the contagious care that comes from such a sense of community."

The chorus of "Friends of the Family" recognizes this community of caring as the remedy for the sense of isolation that can come with being confined to a hospital room:

I met some friends of the family

Love can build a home away from home

I met some friends of the family

Friends among the best I've ever known

The bridge to the song perfectly captures how small acts of kindness may be all it takes to start a new healing relationship:

Did you ever notice when you feel brand-new

You don't know them and they don't know you

You wonder how you're ever gonna break the ice

Then someone comes along and treats you kinda nice, like

Friends of the family

Friends among the best I've ever known

Jill Koss, director of Family Support Services at Cook Children's Medical Center in Fort Worth, Texas, described how the KidLinks songs and sing-along experiences helped a young leukemia patient deal with his illness and treatment. "He had been recently diagnosed, still having major issues with procedures, being combative and angry. I remember giving a *Friends of the Family* cassette tape to his dad and telling him he needed to play it on their long drive home and on their way back. When his son came into the playroom for a sing-along when Jim was there, he knew almost every song lyric."

"The thing that was most impactful, though, was that he stopped fighting with procedures and he was able to cope. Can you relate that change specifically to that music? No. But over this six-month period, nothing else had changed in his life, and he really turned it around and was able to sit still during procedures. I think, for him, music was one of those things that helped him."

"Friends of the Family" celebrates the positive human response to others in need. It tells children and caregivers who are suffering through an illness that they are not alone. The song reminds listeners that everyone is connected, and that when others within our community are hurting, everyone feels their pain. According to Jim, "We have always seen this song as an affirmation for the entire healing community. Family members, patients, hospital staff—even therapeutic musicians like us—come together to try to help a child have a better life despite their illness."

"HOSPITAL RAP" (CREATING FUN AND DISTRACTION)

The adage "Laughter is the best medicine" is based on the belief that mood impacts the healing process. Laughing contributes to both physical and emotional well-being, particularly during life's most difficult challenges.

That is certainly what Patch Adams believed when he entered the field of medicine in the 1980s. He sought to change medical practices that dehumanized patients by treating them as subjects devoid of hopes, dreams, and emotions. His goal was to change the system by challenging the prevailing medical practices by which patients did not need to be engaged but simply needed treatment.

In a scene early in the 1993 self-titled movie, medical student Patch Adams visits a room full of pediatric cancer patients. He fakes exaggerated physical responses to a reflex hammer, dons a bedpan as a hat, inflates rubber gloves into balloons, and converts a red rubber enema bulb into a clown nose, all to the delight of his audience. Bedridden children watch and laugh at Patch's pratfalls and, for a few brief minutes, are taken away from their pain and disease where they feel like children again, not patients defined by their diseases.

When a colleague challenges Patch on the efficacy and appropriateness of entertaining the children with humor, he replied,

"They brighten up for a brief moment. They don't concentrate on the pain. They don't even feel the pain."

Jim and Paul did not have the benefit of knowing about Patch Adams's pioneering efforts to bring humor into hospitals when they started to write music for severely ill children. Neither did they receive any explicit direction from the experts regarding the potential utility of songs that contained humor to offer distraction from illness. They viewed humor as an element of song style rather than a specific need. According to Paul, "We assumed all children's music needed to contain playful elements, so we built that into many of our early songs."

One such song, titled "Fuzzy Wuzzy," was written by Noel with the help of members of a songwriting class in 1999. Noel's spouse, Betty, had taken a position as chaplain at the Northfield Mount Hermon prep school in Massachusetts, where Noel agreed to teach a class on songwriting. One day, Noel started the class by writing these lines on the blackboard:

Fuzzy Wuzzy was a bear

Fuzzy Wuzzy had no hair

Fuzzy Wuzzy wasn't very fuzzy, was he?

The students were given the assignment to write two additional verses using the same rhyme scheme. Their work produced verses about two new characters (Busy Izzy and Squishy Fishy) in addition to a chorus. Noel, Jim, and Paul felt that this fun tune would be a good addition to their growing category of fun songs. "Fuzzy Wuzzy" was recorded for the Parents' Choice Award–winning album titled *World around Song.*

Jim recalled the first time he and Paul heard the song. "We just loved it. Laughter is one of God's greatest gifts, and anything we can do to reconnect people with it, particularly under stressful circumstances, is a good thing."

Another song intended to create fun and distraction was "Hospital Rap." This original composition of Jim's was indirectly inspired by results of a 1986 survey with Association for the Care of Children's Health (ACCH) members. These experts indicated music might benefit children by helping them process the many dimensions and directions of their anger: at their sickness, toward God, and at the medical procedures, staff, and obscure acronyms they encountered. One child life specialist suggested using the hospitalized child's voice in the song, which is what Jim did in this verse of "Hospital Rap":

> **I wanna go home to see my old friends**
> **But the testin' and the treatin', they seem to never end**
> **I guess I'd better stay 'til they get me checked out**
> **But once in a while it makes me want to shout**

Jim added a single-line chorus that repeats multiple times throughout the song and sums up how children may view their treatment and hospital experience:

> **Doctor, doctor, I know you want to help but sometimes it hurts**

"When I came up with the line, my intention was to allow child patients to express their fear and pain and discomfort flowing from medical procedures they have to endure in order to try to get well," said Jim. "Given the power doctors had back in the eighties, and perhaps to a lesser but still significant extent today, kids and even parents might find it difficult to express their disgruntled feelings to medical staff. I wanted to give them a voice."

On a few occasions, doctors interpreted the line as suggesting that medical staff intentionally hurt their pediatric patients. Jim would explain that the lyrics certainly didn't have such intent. The concept behind "Hospital Rap" was to allow children to talk back in an innocent manner about the peculiar language and sometimes painful treatment routines they encountered during hospitalization.

Sung over a driving rap beat, the verses parody the language and acronyms prevalent in the medical world:

> **I never did hear so many funny names**
> **If I can't keep 'em straight, you know I'm not to blame**
> **PICU, NICU, MICU, SICU**
> **Cath lab, Rehab, Radiology**
> **Sometimes I don't know Where I'm supposed to be**

RN, LVN, Child Life, volunteer
Dr. This and Dr. That, a lab tech, an RT
You never can tell
Just who you might see
Cat Scan, EKG, EEG, IV
IVP, Porta Cath, UGI, BP
They do so many things
Just to try to help me

As was the case for Patch Adams's use of humor, it took time for the medical establishment to appreciate and accept the role that fun and distraction could play during hospitalization. (Medical school officials criticized Dr. Adams for his "excessive happiness.") But Jim and Paul quickly noticed how the spirit of the song's rap beat could energize their young audiences. "One day we played in a clinic for cancer and blood disorders where two little children and their mothers were sitting close to us," said Jim. "The boy was doing some artwork, and the girl, who was very frail and had lost her hair from chemotherapy, was being cuddled by her mom. We barely got into 'Hospital Rap' when the little boy came alive! He jumped down on the floor and started spinning around and around like a top, legs and arms going every which-a-way! The little girl then stood up and started shaking her rhythm shakers and swaying to the music."

In a letter to Jim, another mother shared the emotive value her son gained from the song. "We played your tape on the way home after each chemotherapy session. Now I hear my son singing snatches of songs while he plays, especially, 'Doctor, doctor, I know you want to help but sometimes it hurts.' Your music has helped him cope with the changes in his life that leukemia has brought."

The child life community certainly understood why "Hospital Rap" was a favorite among pediatric patients. According to one child life specialist, "'Hospital Rap' portrays what a kid is going through well. 'Doctor, doctor, I know you want to help but sometimes it hurts' is such a good line. This song is my all-time favorite because it covers every inch of what a kid might see in the hospital, whether it's cancer or a simple asthma attack. It is such a good, therapeutic, fun song."

"IF I COULD" (OFFERING COMFORT)

We all recognize the power of lullabies—classic songs used for generations to calm and comfort little children. While there may be no replacement for a mother's soothing voice to comfort a sick child, through thousands of hospital visits Jim and Paul learned that the right song offered in a sensitive manner could work wonders.

Jim recalled playing a song of comfort for a small child and his mother. "A little two-year-old had been crying and screaming in his hospital crib for hours. According to his nurse, nothing would calm him. As I approached his door, I could hear the fear and anger in his voice. When I entered the room, he looked at me and began crying louder than ever.

"I began to play and sing softly a few feet from his bed. At first, there was no change. But then he began to breathe more deeply between cries in order to hear what I was singing. By the middle of the song, he was breathing more and crying less. Toward the end of the song, he just looked at me with sleepy eyes and plopped over sideways onto the pillow. I kept playing and singing that lullaby until he closed his eyes as I slipped out of the room."

Jim and Paul identified two important elements needed for a song of comfort to connect with its audience: sensitive lyrics that could evoke an emotional response from adults combined with a soothing melody capable of relaxing little children. Jim recalled one visit to a hospital in Greenville, South Carolina, where music's capacity to calm was recognized. "We were going to one of their NICUs [newborn intensive care units] where they are very protective of the kids. A doctor there said, 'This is the most wonderful thing I have heard. You can play for all my babies.' We ended up staying about twice as long as we expected, singing some of our soft songs. There is a sense of comfort that music brings to at-risk situations that helps everyone, including the doctors and staff."

One experience that has been repeated on countless occasions is when a song designed to comfort the child induced a spontaneous expression of emotion, usually in the form of tears, from an adult. Jim recalled the time he played a song for a two-year-old and his grandmother. "She immediately began tearing up. It wasn't 'boo-hoo,' but she was really crying and the tears were coming. She was in so much pain and maybe wasn't able to express it, but the song gave her an outlet. I guess when a song connects with the hearts of people it becomes whatever it needs to be for them. People bring their pain to this healing source that is music."

Paul composition "If I Could" delivers a caring message via a comforting melody. Written in first person, each verse expresses in a pleading fashion the singer's desire to make things better for another person through the gift of a song, through friendship, or even a simple smile. But as is so often the case in KidLinks songs, the bridge says it all:

And if I could
I would stop the pain from ever getting through
I would keep this world from ever hurting you
If I could

The emotional power of "If I Could" comes from lyrics that accurately capture the dedication and love parents feel when their child is very ill but may not be able to express in the situation.

Reactions from child life specialists who reviewed "If I Could" spoke to the power of Paul's lyrics. One wrote, "Good for telling kids you love them and care even though you don't always have control of what's going on with them." Another said, "Beautiful. Great listening. It also captures the feeling of helplessness of nurses or parents who wish they could do something."

Paul had originally written "If I Could" for a different reason without realizing how well it addressed the need for songs of comfort in the hospital context. According to Paul, "This is unusual because it was written for my sister-in-law for her birthday. Her neighbor said, 'Karen loves your music. I will commission you to write her a song as my gift to her.' That's where the first line, 'If I could,' comes from.

So I thought about what else you might say that was being nice to someone. Later, when we started gathering songs, I brought out my old notebooks and said, 'Look at this.' It kind of came in the side door."

"This is a perfect song for a completely different set of circumstances than Paul's original assignment," said Jim. "We hope to take away the pain for all the children and adults we play for. It was as if it was written for that purpose."

"If I Could" communicates the intrinsic human desire to be there and to comfort and help others during their time of need by containing meaningful messages able to connect with even the toughest of audiences. Paul recalled a room visit where he and Jim sang one of these songs of comfort. "We went into a room where there was a young father with his daughter.

The father wore baggy shorts, had tattoos, and his cap was on backward. I assumed he was a tough guy, or at least that is what he wanted to appear to be. He was facing away from us, holding his daughter's hand very tenderly. We played our song, and he stroked her hand. As we finished, he turned around and he had tears in his eyes. He thanked us."

Paul continued, "There is something about this crisis situation that levels the playing field. In some sense, tragedy and hardship help us to see each other eye to eye. There is something about music's ability to open up our common humanity to say that, beneath it all, we really are all the same. It is like shaking hands across the great void."

Jim summarized the beliefs underlying the service and mission of KidLinks in this way: "In crisis situations, we must face our human frailty and mortality. Sickness is especially threatening when it is a child who is seriously ill. We know we cannot change or fix or control matters, but we can offer comfort."

"LIFE IS ALOHA" (HELPING TO REMEMBER)

Jim first recognized the need for songs of remembrance during his visits to summer camps attended by children hoping to recover from severe illnesses. Jim wrote "Life Is Aloha" at Camp Star Trails in South Texas. "For many years, we did a memorial service at the camp. I always thought it was so interesting that 'aloha' meant both hello and goodbye. I saw it as a good metaphor for life and death."

Jim also understood how "Life Is Aloha" might be relevant when played in the hospital. "When kids go to the hospital, they have to say goodbye to their home, their pets, their school, their friends. But soon they say hello to a caring community. And then when they leave the hospital, it may be hard to say goodbye to their hospital family and to say hello again to their home. So, in this song, I was trying to say that an important life skill is learning how to say hello and goodbye."

Perhaps no person understood the power and relevance of this song more than Dr. Robert Krout, former director of the Music Therapy Department at Southern Methodist University (SMU) in Dallas. Dr. Krout ran a bereavement camp in Florida during the 1990s where he discovered KidLinks songbooks as he was going through materials that his predecessor had left behind. He liked "Life Is Aloha" so much it became the theme for the camp. Years later, when he first met Jim, Dr. Krout immediately sat down at the piano and sang the song for him.

Set to a gentle waltz rhythm, the lyrics to each verse express the connected nature of hellos and goodbyes:

> **Each hello must have a goodbye**
> **Somewhere down the line**
> **But we know after every goodbye**
> **There's a new hello not far behind**
>
> **Some goodbyes may seem to last**
> **Forever and a day**
> **But our memories and faith remind us**
> **Even this will fade away**

According to Dr. Krout, "It's a really poignant song. Like a lot of Jim and Paul's music, there are a lot of levels to it. 'Aloha' as a word for both hello and goodbye can validate that life has beginnings and life has endings. For our kids at bereavement camp, the endings might be when a loved one died and the beginning of a new journey without that loved one. Or it could be that coming to camp, even just for a few days, where all the other kids there had a loved one die, helps them not feel funny there. Then, at the end of this incredibly bonding camp experience, they have to leave, and they can be grieving over that loss. It's really interesting because it's not like there is one beginning and one ending, but there are all of these beginnings and endings. This song captures it all in a single word that means two things."

That is precisely what Jim was trying to say in the song's chorus:

Aloha—hello
Aloha—goodbye
Life is a circle
We go 'round together
Hello and goodbye

Jim learned through feedback from parents just how meaningful "Life Is Aloha" could be in the hospital and how its core message remained meaningful afterward. One mother wrote, "I want to thank you for your visit to the PICU [pediatric intensive care unit]. You sang to my son extra loud since he was sedated and on a noisy respirator. Sadly, he died a few weeks later, but I am glad that he left with a song in his heart. I have listened over and over to 'Life Is Aloha,' and it brings me much comfort. We even played it at his memorial ceremony."

Another song Jim wrote that was rooted in the summer camp experience became a regular request for use in memorial services. Located in Central Texas, Peaceable Kingdom Retreat for Children provides children suffering from chronic illnesses or facing special needs a place to get away from hospitals and enjoy nature. Named after the camp, "Peaceable Kingdom" has a chorus that describes a longing to go to this destination:

I want to go there to see old and make new friends
I want to go there, to a place where healing love never ends
Where your spirit will be fed
And there's a place to rest your head and heart

The brilliance of "Peaceable Kingdom" is how its two verses operate on different levels. The first verse describes daily life at the camp:

In the Peaceable Kingdom, we will sing and laugh and play

In the Peaceable Kingdom, we will fully live this day

And when evening falls and our bodies call for the healing rest we need

We'll dream of bright tomorrows

In the Peaceable Kingdom

However, the second verse, inspired by Isaiah 11:16, uses the camp setting as a metaphor for eternal life after death:

The Peaceable Kingdom a child will lead the way

To the Peaceable Kingdom, and the lion and the lamb will play

And our trust will grow as we come to know the treasures of each new day

And the promise of forever

In the Peaceable Kingdom

One of the more powerful stories about this song comes from Jill Koss, director of Family Support Services at Cook Children's Medical Center. "We had a little guy from West Texas who had been in and out of the hospital for a long, long time and was very familiar with Jim's music. He was at a point where he was actively dying. He couldn't come down to the playroom, and the mom had asked specifically for Jim to play in his room where he sang 'Peaceable Kingdom.' The song was very impactful for this mom. Sometimes, at the end of the day, that's all you are left with is the words and the feelings that come from those words. For that mom, that's what she had—the words from that song."

Hospital chaplains come to understand that no matter how sick their offspring may be, parents are never prepared for a child's death. But Jim's experience singing both "Life Is Aloha" and "Peaceable Kingdom" provided him with insight into how music can be helpful as part of a family's grieving process. "These songs are meant to provide a sense of comfort during a time of grief. They help comfort people who have lost a child and prepare parents who may lose a child in the hospital because they say there is something beyond this earthly world."

Jim and Paul were surprised at first to find songs written to provide comfort and express hope also had a meaningful impact when sung at memorial services honoring the memory of a lost child. But when considered in light of the KidLinks goal to create a new genre of therapeutic music for severely ill children and their caregivers, the application seems obvious. "Our job is to provide songs to help bring some sense of meaning to something that is beyond words, which is a lot of what music does anyway," said Jim. "We try to bring some positive meaning with the words, and what can't be covered with words is covered by the tones. It is just a matter of bringing comfort with soft music and words that somehow touch their pain."

CHAPTER SIX

Art of the Heart

Noel called the music the KidLinks team was creating "art of the heart." The phrase conjures up images of folk music, the genre that Noel and his bandmates Peter and Mary were instrumental in popularizing in the 1960s. Like folk music, the songs Jim and Paul and Noel produced were intended to impact the lives of the listeners. But what exactly are the defining characteristics that qualify KidLinks therapeutic music for children to be called "art of the heart"?

Attempting to define any genre of music is risky, because written words cannot fully capture the sound and intent. Nevertheless, KidLinks therapeutic music for children can best be defined as a unique blend of four characteristics: the *messages* the songs contain, the *method* by which they are developed, the *manner* in which are arranged, and the *motivation* behind making them.

MESSAGES CONTAINED

It was Jim's powerful insight that, in order to bring the healing power of music to severely ill children, his songs needed to deliver appropriate messages. Aware of his limited understanding regarding the plight of hospitalized children, he listened to the experts. "We asked people who worked every day with kids who have special emotional and physical needs how they felt, what their dilemmas were, and what messages and styles of music would be supportive of them."

One of Jim's most valued resources became Chris Brown, child life director at Hassenfeld Children's Hospital at NYU Langone Medical Center, who described to Jim the hospital experience from a child's point of view. "In the hospital, kids feel powerless. They have little say in what happens to them. They learn pretty early that the adults are the ones who make all the decisions, so anytime they can express what it is like to be a child facing those challenges, they don't feel completely crushed by the experience."

To learn more about the challenges children and their families face during hospitalization, Jim attended the annual Association for the Care of Children's Health (ACCH) conference in May 1985. He received permission to mail a survey to one thousand random members to gather feedback from its broad spectrum of family-centered healthcare professionals: doctors, nurses, administrators, child life experts, social workers, and music therapists. The questionnaire asked about music resources currently being used in hospitals and the most critical emotional areas new songs might address.

The solid response rate indicated a high degree of interest in the subject. Out of the 334 respondents who returned the survey, most affirmed the value therapeutic music could provide for severely ill children. Many unsolicited words of encouragement poured forth, an indication that Jim was on the right track. Comments included,

> **"Great idea! Any work on empowering children in the hospital is very valuable."**
> **"This type of project is much needed."**
> **"Good idea. Nothing like it out there."**

The results were nourishment for a team seeking deep insight into the needs of their target audience. By identifying the spectrum of feelings children can experience when hospitalized, Jim and Paul gained a better sense of the emotional challenges their music needed to address:

- Competence/mastery ("I can do more than I can't")

- Self-esteem ("I am still me")

- Fear of abandonment or medical procedures ("I am really scared")

- Anger (at the sickness, at doctors and nurses, at procedures, at God)

- Hopelessness ("Will I ever get better?")

- Guilt ("Look what I'm putting my family through")

- Loneliness (missing friends, pets, family routines)

- Feeling expression ("I don't know how to talk about what is happening")

This rich range of topics provided material for their songwriting efforts for years to come.

METHOD OF DEVELOPMENT

While Jim had learned a great deal from his interviews with child life specialists, he believed expert input was needed to guide the team's work throughout the song creation process.

"From the beginning, we used a method to make sure what we did was helpful," Jim explained. "We put a process in place that would help guide our work from initial idea through final song production. Everything grew out of the feedback we got."

Jim and Paul began to translate what they learned into songs containing messages these children and their families needed to hear. The process was not always easy for songwriters accustomed to writing about topics and themes important to them personally. In order to increase the odds of developing songs that accomplished their intent, they implemented a way to gain input on emerging song concepts. "Once we had a few songs recorded, we would present them to the child life experts for feedback," recalled Jim. It was a logical way to improve each song and reduce the chances of moving forward with a song that was not sensitive to the needs they hoped it would address.

Jim and Paul were seeking that kind of input at the ACCH conference in 1987 during a workshop titled "Music for Children in Healthcare Situations," where they shared twenty song concepts and invited attendee input. This simple act of asking for feedback surprised and inspired many there. "You mean you will actually change a song?" one asked.

Jim's and Paul's openness to input and feedback spoke to their commitment to making sure their songs achieved the goal of being helpful and therapeutic. Still, they occasionally found the feedback difficult to accept. "Sometimes the process of checks and balances we put in place—having a review board made up of child life specialists—felt like 'creativity by committee,' which seldom works," said Jim. "There were times when my most clever lyric got axed because they thought it might have inappropriate interpretations by the children. I found it frustrating."

However, the process allowed great work to unfold. "As we wrote, we would occasionally forget our target audience and include a verse adults would understand but that kids didn't get," said Jim. "The experts had to keep pulling us down into the appropriate age range.

You have to get your ego out of the way as a writer because you get critiqued, as well you should."

MANNER IN WHICH THEY WERE ARRANGED

The third defining characteristic of KidLinks therapeutic music is the *manner* in which these important messages were arranged into songs. For the messages to be heard, the lyrics needed to be simple enough for children to relate to and enjoy. Noel described this quality as "musical accessibility"—the use of language and images that could be easily understood and assimilated. This required avoiding words or figures of speech that were beyond the reach of the youngest children. "I wanted our music to be a place where, regardless of level of musical ability, you could access and immerse yourself in the content," said Noel.

Jim, Paul, and Noel believed the song arrangements needed to be able to attract and hold the interest of children and adults, which meant retaining the playfulness that characterizes children's music while also including clever elements pleasing to listeners of all ages across multiple exposures. As Noel put it, "We make an effort to delight parents, not just so their kids will like it but so they can endure the presentation. We try to create surprises. I think the appreciation of KidLinks music is on many levels. There is lyric content. There is an aural content. What we have always tried to do is select arrangements that suited what the song was trying to say. It is not just to make it pretty music."

MOTIVATION BEHIND MAKING

The fourth defining characteristic of art of the heart is the *motivation* behind it. The music was born out of the desire to provide songs that were helpful to children as well as their families facing the toughest of situations. KidLinks' songs are purposeful and other-directed— concerned about what they provide the audience and not what they produce for the writers. The focus is unwavering. According to one child life director in a major children's hospital, "Each song is written and produced with a child in mind. That is the beauty of their unique music."

This purposeful motivation touched Noel's heart and fueled his ongoing involvement. It reminded him of the selfless ethic of folk music he became aware of from Peter and Mary. "I learned from my partners and from this legacy of folk music that there are many different motives for writing music. I think it was Peter who said to me, 'These songs we are doing were not written for money. They were written because they were talking about issues that needed to be spoken of.' More and more my heart was drawn to these songs of the heart, these expressions of earnest conviction, earnest care, a desire for equity, the desire to make the world a better place than when we arrived. As that ethic grew in me, I left music for entertainment purposes behind me and joined a brigade of people who write from conviction and because there is a need for the communication of some purpose."

These comments mirror Jim's original motivation and mission. His goal was not merely to make pleasing music but to create music that had a positive impact. "When I look at much of the music that Paul and Jim have created, it's obviously not created to make a dollar," said Noel. "It's created to make a difference in a child's life."

Art of the heart was about creating musical experiences that went beyond the inherent therapeutic value of music. Because KidLinks therapeutic music for children used a method that placed a premium on the emotional needs of the child, the songs contained thoughtful but easily understandable lyrics carrying messages these children needed to hear. The songs were carefully arranged to allow easy access to those messages in an engaging manner that would capture and retain the attention of the listener. The underlying motivation was not to gain fame or fortune but to help children get through their medical challenges.

KidLinks music, at its most basic, is music for those who are hurting. It's simple music that expresses healing messages these children need to hear. KidLinks music's timeless appeal is based on its helpful messages made accessible through simple yet interesting arrangements. It's created to serve others rather than for commercial appeal. In a sense, KidLinks music achieves at the micro level what folk music does for communities: it expresses the current realities in order to define and reach a better future.

Noel is proud of the role he played in creating what he called "art of the heart." As Noel said, "We have learned that the central core mission of KidLinks is not about just making music. It's not about being successful in the world's eyes because we constantly want to keep our anchor line tied to the original premise: is this making a difference in a child's life?"

These four defining characteristics explain how the therapeutic music Jim had in mind was able to achieve the quality ideal he established from the very beginning. "We were always committed to the quality of the sound of the song, the quality of the composition, and the quality of the truth," said Jim.

Perhaps the most important recognition came from child life experts who continue to play a critical role in the song creation process. As child life specialist Chris Brown said, "The songs they have written and recorded are so appropriate for kids in the hospital because the messages are so rare in children's music. The messages around self-esteem and healing and taking things 'one day at a time' and being 'the best you can be' really are the messages the kids in the hospital desperately need to hear."

CHAPTER SEVEN

In The Playroom

The words sound familiar, but their meanings are different. In The Playroom, conversations are laced with terms like patches and scratches, pickups and grooves, tracks and keys. It could lead one to think they have wandered into an auto body shop instead of a recording studio.

Paul and Jim invited the team here in May 2013 to record five new songs. Prior albums received a number of prestigious awards—like Parent's Choice and an American Library Association Notable Children's Recording recognition—so they had a high standard to uphold. Paul was responsible for organizing the session and selecting the musicians in consultation with Noel. Having two days of Noel's time was a luxury, so Paul recruited the best talent he could find to complete the work.

Denny Bouchard, a longtime friend of Noel, would handle keyboards. He had left Maine in his twenties and headed to California in search of a dream. "I didn't want to play music. I wanted to make it." In addition to his skills playing a keyboard loaded with a digital library of instrument sounds, Denny provided the team with a blend of incisive analysis, creative input, and constant playfulness, like his "Out-of-Time Polka" played during one break.

George Anderson, described by one member of the team as "offensively good," would handle the bass. Milo Deering would show up late on the second day to add finishing touches to their work with fiddle, Dobro, or mandolin, depending on which instrument he judged best fit the song. Joel Cameron rounded out the lineup, playing the dual roles of studio engineer and percussionist. He would be responsible for all aspects of capturing sounds and then assembling the resulting mosaic of tracks into a final recording. Joel also owned and operated The Playroom—so named because, according to him, "it is a place where people come to play."

Noel was there to oversee the recording process, acting as maestro for the small ensemble. At the fundraising concert on behalf of KidLinks the day before, he had characterized the creation of a song in terms similar to Michelangelo's description of the sculptor's role as one of removing that which surrounds what already exists. By trusting in the process and the assembled talent, Noel believed something very good would emerge from their work together. With Noel and Paul in charge of artistic direction, it always did.

*****

The Playroom studio is located in the scrubland between Murphy and Wylie, Texas. Until about twenty years ago, these were two small towns located about fifteen miles northeast of downtown Dallas. Today, countless shopping options cover land where cattle once grazed. The cows have been replaced by human creatures who roam from one retail establishment to the next, herded into drive-through lines of a dizzying array of fast-food options.

The studio lies hidden deep inside an unassuming building outside of Wylie. A family member convinced the owner to allow him to place his studio equipment in a room in the heart of the building. Joel later bought the equipment from the family and established a long-term rental agreement for the space. (The existence of this oasis within this structure makes one wonder what other secret enterprises might be hiding inside the similar Morton industrial buildings located nearby.)

The studio is a large rectangular space bisected at an angle with a glass wall in the middle, producing two trapezoid-shaped rooms. On one side sits "mission control," comprising recording equipment, digital screens, and speakers. One sofa and a couple of lounge chairs sit wedged along the wall perimeter.

The heart of the system, the soundboard, contains over twenty columns with over twenty buttons on each. On the other side of the window are microphones and an assortment of drum options where musicians being recorded can be isolated from any ambient noise. The large window on the slanted wall facilitates an unobstructed view from each side of what is happening on the other.

No natural light penetrates this building inside a building. An occasional rumble sneaks past the soundproof walls, but for the most part, silence prevails when the musicians are playing and recording. The dark purple walls reinforce the sense of isolation, so much so on the second afternoon of this session the team remained oblivious to severe springtime thunderstorms that rolled through North Texas. Their safety was assured since The Playroom doubles as perhaps the best tornado shelter within miles.

*****

Over the next two days, song concepts would become reality. Abstract notions of what the song would become took shape as the recording and listening begin. Noel's role, in collaboration with Paul, was to maximize the team's creative output by translating each nascent song concept into something special. Everyone on the team was encouraged to participate in the creative exploration of adding and subtracting voices and instruments.

The focus on the first day was laying down the foundation—the bass and drum tracks—for each of the five songs, meaning Joel and George handled most of the instrumental heavy lifting. This critical first step provided the rhythm track against which the other instruments and voices would be added. The kick drum and bass needed to be perfectly in sync before moving to the next stage, since additional voices and instruments would take their cues from these. If the two instruments were even the slightest bit off, the other musicians might focus on one or the other while adding their tracks, compounding the error. According to Jim, "It's like a building, everything falls apart if the foundation is not solid."

Vocals and additional instruments were the primary focus on the second day. During early takes, the singers recorded what are called "scratch vocals," which provide the team a sense for the overall sound of the song and to assist in keeping track of where they are in a song. These would be replaced later once the other elements of the song had been established. In the days and weeks ahead, vocal refinements like adding the voices of a children's choir or doing touch-up work on issues identified later with the lead track would be completed.

Finalizing the vocals can be the most tedious and repetitive part of the recording process. The human voice possesses almost unlimited potential for slight yet powerful variations, and the human ear is able to detect these subtle differences in vocal expression. Changing the emphasis, enunciation, and color of the voice can drastically impact the overall feel of the song.

Noel played the role of vocal choreographer throughout. He instructed Jim to "move a syllable forward" when he sang the word "shouldn't" by pronouncing it as "shood-ant." Articulation tips like this may feel exaggerated and over the top, but Noel had learned they help the listener hear the intended lyrics even though they are not pronounced exactly how we might enunciate them in normal conversation.

Digital equipment has changed what is possible compared to when the team members first began recording decades earlier. These veteran musicians were eager to adapt to the digital world because small changes are now possible without needing to make another complete recording, rendering the process more efficient. For example, during the initial foundation work on one song, Denny noted a timing discrepancy between the bass and the kick drum, something an ordinary listener would miss. Like volleys in a tennis match, opinions shot back and forth regarding which instrument might be the culprit. To resolve the debate, Joel scanned the horizontal lines of sound waves representing each track to isolate the exact location of the problem. With current editing capabilities, he slid the single note from the bass forward to align it with the drum. Problem solved.

The same technology enables re-recording small sections of a song and patching them into the digital file. Even a single bothersome word or note can be fixed. During one take, Noel knew immediately that he had added a note that didn't belong. "I left a clam in there we need to fix. You need to do some magic there, Joel." Jim called this digital erasing of the problem from the track and their memory a "note-ectomy." Revisions no longer require a complete retake by all the musicians. Instead, the engineer is able to remake the song bit by tiny bit.

*****

The five songs the team worked on were chosen using the approach Jim and Paul used for their previous albums. For this project, demo versions of thirteen songs were sent to a panel of child life specialists for their input. The final selections were based on their ratings on a five-point likeability scale and open-ended comments. Jim, Paul, and Noel combined this feedback with a good dose of their personal passions and judgment to arrive at the priorities for the recording session.

The highest-scoring song candidate was "Lemme Be Your Friend," an homage to the composer's canine companion. The team had recorded it earlier that year, so their current work began with David Mallett's "Garden Song." While it received positive reviews from the experts surveyed, Jim and Paul were concerned that the number had already been recorded by too many other artists, including Peter, Paul and Mary. But Noel insisted it be part of the current project. A compromise was reached through the decision to append it with a new composition about small critter friends by Bob Payne titled "All in Your Backyard."

Another song on their list was one about the relationships between humans and nature titled "Everything You Touch," which would be supported by a reggae beat because, as Denny said, "Who doesn't like reggae?" They would also tackle Paul's musical conversation about diversity and inclusiveness titled "It Wouldn't Be a Zoo without You," a song that would test their abilities and patience with its varying time signatures. For "Cotton Candy Clouds," the lullaby written for his daughters, Jim recorded a vocal track against which Denny would add a synthesized harp accompaniment in his personal studio at a later date. The final song they would record was another composition by Paul called "Just One."

Paul, Noel, Jim, and Denny had met on Saturday to chart a general creative direction for each song. That did not mean that each song was scored and scripted in detail. Perhaps 80 percent of the arrangement was defined in advance. In the studio, they embarked in that general direction while leaving ample room for exploration. One suggestion led to another. Sometimes the idea moved the song forward while others were rejected once they listened to the work. Not exactly trial and error, the approach might be more aptly described as "experiment and experience." The outcome was unpredictable but the results were usually delightful. According to Noel, "We plan our randomness."

While the approach was organic in nature, a basic series of steps was followed for each song. First, the team listened to the demo version, taking mental and written notes. After a brief discussion regarding areas where clarity of direction was needed, the group might play through the song together. Once they felt comfortable with the song (which for these professionals required only one or two times through), an initial recording was made starting with the foundation. The act of recording raised the stakes and revealed trouble spots. Some songs came together quickly while others seemed to resist the team's efforts to tame them. But Noel remained a voice of optimism, encouraging the team each step along the way. "We'll figure it out," he said to assure the team and himself.

Even professional musicians can stumble over the unique language of their trade. While listening to an initial recording of one song, an interchange reminiscent of an Abbott-and-Costello dialogue ensued:

"There's some seafood in there," said Denny, usually the first to recognize a problem.

"Yes," said Noel. "I had a finger fart in there. The one happens on the four and I think I lost it."

"Yes, you rushed it a little," agreed Denny.

"I'm not sure you are talking about the same thing," said Joel, trying to help cut through the confusion. "Are you talking harmonically or rhythmically?" he asked, hoping to get to the heart of the matter. (The misunderstanding stemmed from their use of the same numeric shorthand to describe two different dimensions of music. When used to describe the chord progression of a piece, referred to by some as the Nashville Number System, "IV" refers to the chord of the fourth step of the scale above the key in which the song is written. For example, if a song is written in the key of G, that chord would be referred to as the "I" while C would be the "IV." However, rhythmically, the "4" might refer to the fourth beat in a measure.)

Noel cleared up the confusion. "I was talking about the IV chord." Joel shook his head. "There are just too many numbers in music."

Inside The Playroom, Noel set the agenda and pace, facilitating an open creative process where differences of opinion were shared in the spirit of making the work better. The session became Noel's musical playground, a place where he was overflowing with new ideas but also encouraged everyone to offer their opinion on any aspect of the recording. Try a verse a cappella? Add more drums? Drop out one of the voices or instruments? There were endless possibilities, and the team searched out the best ones to see how well they fit.

For this free-flowing approach to succeed, immense trust between all of the players was required. Each member was expected to both offer his suggestions and entertain the ideas of others. The common goal was to move the song concept to its best possible result. It was a collective effort where the outcome was greater than the sum of the individual parts.

For example, as they listened to their initial recording of "Garden Song," Joel commented, "It feels too exposed. It needs something else." Someone mentioned shakers as a possibility, an idea Noel rejected. "Shakers wouldn't do anything Joel is not doing with the brushes [on the drum]." Denny suggested a half-filled water bottle might work by adding a "swooshing" or "sloshing" noise to the background. Instead, Joel pulled out a Christmas garland he had purchased at Walmart. The "tinselly" sound added a mysterious texture. "It leaves it open but adds some color," said Noel, endorsing the selection. When they listened to the song with it added, everyone loved it. "It sounds like someone is walking through the woods," said Noel. "I love the accidental 'flingle-bangle' that happens here."

After a dinner break at a local BBQ restaurant, the group spent a couple more hours listening to the tracks they had created. The attention to details was unparalleled. Their ears were so well developed that small mistakes a normal listener would miss were obvious to them. After hearing it once they were able to reference specific notes, measures, and phrases where attention was needed. They were not only listening for sonic miscues but also for areas where they could add something to make the song better. They heard what was missing—musical elements that when added would make a difference and take the song to the next level.

For example, in "It Wouldn't Be a Zoo without You," Paul used varying time signatures to dramatize the dialogue between characters in the zoo that occur throughout the song. These transitions proved to be trickier than expected, and the team stumbled over each other as they played through the song the first few times. "I thought this was a children's song," said Noel, acknowledging the irony within their struggle.

But the primary challenge stemmed from the ritards, or moments of silence, in a number of places. Musicians call these "holes," and Denny worked on riffs in an attempt to fill them. During his search, Denny began playing something he said sounded like "a swing version of 'Penny Lane.'" (His admiration for the Beatles seeped through at the most unexpected of moments. He loved their music and talked about the miracle that they came from Liverpool, of all places. He played the introduction to "Strawberry Fields" and declared, "So perfect in color in all of its eight-bit glory.")

After a couple of minutes of focused effort, Denny arrived at a sequence of notes that mirrored an earlier section of the song. The musical voids had been filled in a manner that fit the arrangement. "Music is all about how you deal with the holes," said Denny.

There would be other small adjustments, such as truncating a lyric, replacing guitar chords with arpeggios, or adding color and texture to the vocals, to squeeze a bit more emotion into the lyrics without overwhelming them. The approach was based on the belief that small changes that make the song more interesting and engaging to their ears would do the same for other listeners, even though the latter might never be able to recognize why.

*****

No song reflected the value gained from the input of the child life specialists better than "Just One." Feedback from the review panel guided a significant overhaul of the lyrics. In its original demo recording, Paul used the metaphor of "one thread" to introduce the message. Starting with the assertion that a single fiber "can't do much" on its own, the verse described how something so small and singular can become something remarkable when combined with others.

> **The number will just keep on growing**
> **And there's just no way of knowing what that one might become**
> **Maybe a shirt or a pair of pants or a robe for a mighty king**
> **Just one thread and a few score more**
> **Might become most anything Oh, ho. You never know**

The experts endorsed the overall message about the potential to accomplish the unexpected through collaboration, but many expressed concerns that the sewing metaphor might be too abstract for the younger audiences to understand and appreciate. "It may be a bit hard to follow." "Younger ones may not grasp the thread concept." In response to the feedback, Paul not only addressed these concerns in his revisions, he also created a stronger set of lyrics.

While the child life specialists guided the messaging, the musicians oversaw the creative evolution from a solid piece of music into an exceptional song. The version on the demo recording was against a simple and unassuming melody. At the planning meeting the night before the recording session, the team agreed the studio execution should reflect a zydeco feel. Paul had this in mind when he wrote the song in 4/4 time using only major chords. This artistic direction gave Denny license to explore his musical library to locate ways his keyboard could express the signature accordion sound.

The initial attempt at a recording revealed that a synchronized start to the song was elusive because bare vocals introduced the first verse with no rhythm track. The lyrics begin,

I found a block . . . made of wood
Just one block is not much good

The instruments should enter after that second line, but the group tripped over the chord progression and timing. "It's I, V, I," said Paul, referring to the chord progression. "You vamp on the I at the start," he continued. After a couple of false starts, they succeeded in laying down a track that they could build upon.

The discussion then turned to the number and types of instruments to include at the start of the song. Since the central concept starts with "just one" of something (whether that be a piece of wood or a friend) to be joined by others, Noel was intrigued with the possibility of reflecting that lyrical concept in the instrumental arrangement. He suggested that the instruments enter sequentially to reinforce the message of working together and growing as a community.

You can't do much with one it's true
But one more one and then there's two

But when they played back their recording, Noel rejected the approach. "It hurts more than it helps," he said.

Listening to the initial recording also revealed that Paul's scratch vocals were too exposed. Something was needed beneath the vocals to prevent it from sounding too naked. After brainstorming options, Joel pulled a small washboard out of the closet and nominated it for the job. Despite claiming he was not very good at playing it, Joel quickly found a comfortable two-handed rhythm on this folk percussion tool.

"It's great, Joel," said Noel. "It sits beautifully," he added, acknowledging how the washboard served as the perfect complement to the opening vocal lines while setting the tone for the entire song.

"I knew you had some Cajun in you," joked Jim.

At this point, a decision about the vocals was required. Vocal assignments had not been determined in advance, so in situations like this, Noel, Jim, and Paul might each lay down a track so that they could assess whose voice worked best for the song. Since Paul wrote the song and his voice graced the demo, Noel gave him the first crack. But less than halfway through the recording, Noel called it off, feeling Paul's voice was not strong enough to drive the song forward with the added instrumentation.

"Paulie, I think we need Jim's voice on this," he explained.

Paul supported the decision. "I think you'll do a better job, Jim," he said, demonstrating how great musicians leave their egos at the door in order to achieve a better collective result.

Jim's first pass at the vocals was good, but Noel sensed he was pressing too hard. "You're on top of it, Jim. Just relax." In Jim's defense, he had not worked on the song so he was both learning the lyrics and adjusting the syntax on the fly. His second attempt was an improvement, but Noel offered more suggestions. By his fourth run-through, Jim owned the song. At the end of this last take, he celebrated by yodeling, "Aiyeeee!" Everyone liked Jim's spontaneous exclamation point to the song. "What you did is not what I had in mind musically," said Noel, "but I think your version has a stronger emotional feel."

Children's voices would be added at a later date, so the only work that remained on this day on "Just One" was to allow Milo Deering to add sweet instrumental frosting to the musical cake. Although he toured with stars like LeAnn Rimes and Don Henley, Milo was best known for his studio work. The team awaited his arrival with heightened anticipation.

Milo entered The Playroom later that evening with his arsenal of acoustic instruments in tow—fiddle, mandolin, and Dobro. After cordial greetings, he took his position to listen to these songs for the first time and then suggest how he might match the right instrument to each and make it better. While he listened to each song for the first time, he charted his part in a shorthand of the Nashville Number System. His goal was to add color to the recording by determining which of his instruments fit best for each song. In the case of one song, Milo's modesty was exposed when he said they should leave it as is because there was nothing he could add to make it better.

After a single listen to "Just One," Milo suggested adding a fiddle track to the recording. The instrument was consistent with the zydeco feel the team sought and would add energy to the instrumental interlude prior to the bridge in the middle of the song. "I will roll a little bit with this and see what happens," declared Milo. He took his position on the recording side of the glass wall as everyone waited with anticipation. But just as Joel was about to start the recording, Milo called out to Paul, "What key is this in?" He had listened for the relative positions of the chords, which would allow him to adapt his playing to the song regardless of key. "It's in G, Milo," said Paul.

His small audience loved his first attempt. "I'm getting overstimulated," admitted Jim. But Milo believed he could do better. "I'd like to take a couple more swings at it," he said. No one argued. They knew that Milo's focus was on the dynamics of the song—finding ways to improve the finished product without detracting from what was already recorded. On the second pass, he pulled back a bit during the verses, allowing his violin to shine through as the star of the instrumental section. Everyone on the other side of the glass smiled at the beauty and polish of his work. "He could charge admission just to watch him work," said Jim, only partly in jest.

Joel informed Milo that he had enough from the two takes to create the single track they needed. Amazed at how quickly he was able to add his special touches, Denny said, "We've been living these songs for two whole days, and he just walks in and nails it."

Impressed with the understated approach of Milo's work, Noel said, "He is a man of few notes."

"Yes," agreed Jim. "But he plays all the right ones."

*****

As the evening drew to a close and all the instruments were put away, the team returned to the control room. Over the next few days, Joel would make tweaks to the final mix to achieve the desired balance between the tracks. But for now, the current version would provide something they could listen to and assess the music they had created during two days of intense work.

They moved from their seats to stand in a semicircle facing the huge sound board and speakers, their heads were bowed slightly as if before an altar. With their eyes closed to concentrate on the sound, they waited to hear the results of their artistic labor. During one song, Noel nodded his head slightly when he heard something particularly pleasing to his experienced ears.

Finally, the moment arrived for them to hear "Just One," the last song on the master disc Joel had burned. No one had looked forward to this moment more than Paul, who had worked on the song for over a year. He stood behind a chair, his chin resting on folded hands. With each new movement and verse, his smile grew a bit wider and his countenance brighter, like that of a parent experiencing the birth of his child. The final cut was an upbeat, engaging number that made everyone feel good, but no one as much as Paul. His work had come to life.

Liking what they heard, team members exchanged thumbs-up signs and smiles across the room. Noel complimented the entire team on the result. "Great, guys! It's a sweet piece."

Noel looked at Paul and said, "This must be satisfying, Paulie."

"It's kind of like realizing the potential that was in my mind," said Paul. "The feel is perfect."

*****

It was well past nine o'clock at night as they packed up their belongings after consecutive twelve-hour days of work. As they exited The Playroom, they were greeted by north Texas air now cooled by the thunderstorm that had roared through the area while they worked in the silent safety of their studio. Noel, Paul, Jim, Denny, and Joel stood simultaneously exhausted and energized by their work. As they hopped into their cars, Noel announced his approval of their two days together. "Great job, guys. I think it is time for an 'after hours' beverage."

THE DISCIPLINE

CHAPTER EIGHT

Therapeutic Music Entertainment

"No, no, no!" shouted the six-year-old boy from his hospital bed. He was not protesting a shot or the painful poking and prodding he associated with this place. His objection was directed at the two men standing in his room and to their song.

Jim and Paul had arrived at Litta Children's Hospital at the Mayo Clinic in Rochester, Minnesota, to provide their music for the children and families. The child life specialist had suggested they pay a visit to the boy unable to leave his room for the playroom sing-along scheduled later in the day.

After entering his room, the child life specialist asked, "Would you like a song?" The boy hunkered down in his bed a bit, giving Jim the impression of some resistance on the child's part. But his mother was more encouraging. "Give it a try," she said.

Sensing that her son was in no mood for music, Jim replied, "That's fine. We'll just move on to the next room. You have a nice day."

But the mother persisted. "I really think he would like a song. I want you to do a song for him."

Jim and Paul began playing one of the songs they had learned worked well during individual room visits. "I Can Be the Best I Can Be" combines a message of encouragement with playful lyrics and a pleasing melody. But as Jim began to sing the chorus, the boy took his stand.

"No!" he shouted. The strength of his objection stopped the duo midsentence. The mother's face turned beet red, embarrassed that her son may have offended the minstrels. After a few moments of silence, the child sensed his newfound power over the adults and his environment. "Yes!" he shouted. Jim and Paul returned to the song at the precise spot where they had left it.

I can be the best I can be.

I can be. . . .

"No!" shouted the boy in a voice more emphatic than earlier. As Jim and Paul stopped, they looked up to see he was wearing a broad smile, like a child who had opened a present that he had been longing for: the gift of control.

"Yes!" he commanded. This pattern of abrupt starts and stops continued for the next six or seven minutes, more than twice as long as it would normally take to complete this song. When Jim and Paul finished the last chorus, the child was happy as a lark, grinning from ear to ear.

The mother's face was flushed with embarrassment over her son's behavior. "I am so sorry," she said to the duo. "That was so rude."

"That's OK," said Jim. "He doesn't get to control very much here in the hospital. If he wanted to take control of our song, then that was just fine with us."

Had an event like that happened years earlier, Jim and Paul might have taken offense. But through experience they had learned how to navigate the unexpected nuances associated with introducing music into the hospital environment. Allowing a child to refuse a song even if parents gave their consent was one of the first tenets of the disciplined approach to therapeutic music they were creating. In an environment where children can say no to little if anything, honoring their wishes was considered as good a gift as a song might be.

Jim and Paul knew of no precedent for what they were trying to do. There were few guitar players roaming the halls of children's hospitals in search of audiences at the time. Hospital management was just beginning to acknowledge the value of complementary healing modalities like music. The child life discipline was in its early stages, with only the most progressive hospitals having specialists on staff. Family-centered care was an emerging concept. Where the kind of live music Jim and Paul were providing fit into the healthcare equation was anybody's guess.

Their mission "to bring the healing power of music to kids everywhere" demanded more than a series of written and recorded songs. In order to make a difference in the lives of others, Jim believed he must take these songs directly to the audience that most needed to hear them: the children in the hospital. During his earliest visits, Jim found himself in situations where he sensed he might be more in the way than helpful. Nurses were accustomed to executing doctors' orders, and live music was not on the list of prescribed treatment options. Some would ask, "What are you doing here?" Jim would say, "Just here to play some music for the kids." His nonchalant answer was sufficient for most staff because he displayed a genuine sense of caring for the children.

Suspicion and doubt turned into near universal support once the medical staff heard the music and observed the reactions of children and families. Jim's and Paul's voices (and those of other therapeutic music entertainers who represented KidLinks) gave life to their songs' positive messages. But that was only part of it. They presented themselves and their music in a way that was sensitive to the vulnerable position in which these children and their families found themselves.

The music also proved helpful to the nurses. It helped alleviate some of the stress they kept bottled up inside from the parade of suffering they witnessed in their work environment. The music was a nice diversion capable of taking them to an emotional space where they could feel good again.

Jim's and Paul's early visits to children's hospitals provided firsthand experience of the challenges the child life specialists had described to them, revealing at a deeper and more visceral level the harsh realities severely ill children and their families were facing. They saw the impact of hospitalization on not just the child but the entire family. Routines and patterns of normal life were supplanted with unfamiliar faces and procedures. In an environment defined by coercion and chaos, where children exert limited or no control over their world, they may become withdrawn and unable to cope. Jim and Paul understood why that little boy felt compelled to take control of their song from start to finish. His grin at the end was a step toward mastering his own environment, a critical ingredient to enhanced self-esteem.

Each new encounter with either a group of children in a playroom or a visit to a child's private room added to their knowledge about how to maximize the therapeutic and healing value of music experiences with children in clinical settings. It was a disciplined approach that could be codified and taught to others, which they called "therapeutic music entertainment" (TME). Jim defined *therapeutic music entertainment* as "an activity that, by virtue of its diversion, amusement, and/or pleasing qualities, supports and encourages healing." TME incorporates therapeutical and entertainment aspects to address the unique needs of children and their families who are dealing with serious, chronic, and life-threatening illnesses.

According to Jim, "A lot of people say we do music therapy but we don't in the technical sense. We don't have the degree and the training. We are not board-certified. But we've been told by a lot of music therapists that the music we do is therapeutic, so we call ourselves 'therapeutic music entertainers.'"

Music therapists use music in a wide range of healthcare and clinical settings to achieve nonmusical goals such as enhancing memory, improving communication, and promoting physical rehabilitation. During music therapy sessions, the subject produces music under the therapist's guidance to achieve specific objectives defined in advance. In contrast, during a therapeutic music entertainment session, children and their caregivers are the recipients of music, although they sometimes become participants in response to it.

Despite the less structured nature of TME compared to music therapy, many similarities exist. According to Dr. Robert Krout, former head of the Music Therapy Department at Southern Methodist University, "There are a lot of parallels between music therapy and what KidLinks does. [KidLinks uses] precomposed songs of the highest quality on a oneshot basis, trying to reach as many kids as possible. Music therapy uses a wider range of music experiences over an extended time frame. Music therapists who are on staff and are there every day might be doing little things on four days that would allow them to do the really in-depth work on the fifth."

Jim and Paul later learned that TME reflected the origins of music therapy as a discipline. Following World War I, amateur and professional musicians from all walks of life visited hospitals to provide music as a distraction to veterans suffering physical and emotional trauma from the conflict. Doctors noticed the positive responses the music had on overall attitudes and recovery, and hired amateur and professional musicians to play in their hospitals. In 1944, the first official music therapy program started at the Michigan State University to provide appropriate training for those interested in entering this emerging field.

Beyond the fact that music therapy and TME share common roots, both are anchored in the belief that musical activity by its very nature can promote healing. But while music generally possesses properties that are helpful in the hospital due to its capacity to engage attention and amuse, it must be delivered with a sensitivity and understanding of the milieu wherein the children find themselves.

Child life specialists told stories about well-intentioned entertainers who would pay visits to their hospitals. "We get lots of requests from people to come and entertain," said one. "Our philosophy is to make sure that what they do is helpful. Someone who has always performed for adult audiences may not have a lot of skill making it child-focused."

Others told stories about celebrities who appeared to promote themselves and failed to give much thought as to whether their visit was helpful to the patients. Some were so wrapped up in their own reality they were unable to see how an insensitive comment like, "It sure makes you feel lucky that you don't have a kid in here," might have a negative impact on the children and their families.

For the music to be therapeutic in this setting, providers must be intentional about what they are trying to accomplish. Jim and Paul had something going for them that other visiting musicians did not. They possessed a song repertoire that contained helpful messages these children would benefit from hearing. But matching the presenting need of the sick child with the proper song selection required skills that only experience could develop. Someone visiting to "entertain" might leap past this consideration, leaving to chance the potential for a song to have a positive impact.

Selecting the proper song required skills of observation and perception. Age, medical condition, and developmental level offered useful information usually available in advance of the visit. But immediate clues, such as the lighting in the room, were more telling. Pulled shades suggested that something quiet and calm, like a lullaby, might work best. Open shades suggested that something more upbeat might be in order.

Items chosen by the child to be at their side during their hospital stay were also notable. Stuffed animals, blankets, and balloons provided insight into the length of the stay and important emotional connections outside the hospital. The presence of a toy vehicle could help initiate a conversation to introduce a particular song. For example, "If I Had a Truck" connects through verses expressing love through gifts like trucks, cars, and hugs.

The best source of insight into what might be appropriate was the patient. The child's facial expression, skin pallor, posture, and level of consciousness provided a wealth of information. Their alertness level and inclination toward direct eye contact offered windows into their emotional state. Of course, a sleeping child was never interrupted. When in doubt, Jim learned to merely ask, "Would you like something peppy or relaxing?"

The answer would sometimes surprise him. A subdued child just out of surgery might request something a bit more stimulating.

Their ability to match the right song with the child improved with time and experience. Jim and Paul could tell when the right choice was made and the song connected with the child. They frequently received positive feedback, like this comment from a child life specialist:

> **I need to tell you about one patient who was touched in a very special way. This young boy is nine years old and has 20 percent body burns. He would spend much of his time in his bed withdrawing from our attempts to comfort him. Until the day you came and sang to him at his bedside, I had yet to see him relax. You sang the song "If I Could" to him. To this day, he believes it was written just for him.**

One bit of information that helped rule out certain songs, or at least some of the verses, was the patient's diet. KidLinks songs "Inside" and "Wouldn't It" both contain references to food. Mentioning "food" to a child on a restricted diet would be insensitive, so being aware they were on a floor for patients with eating disorders or observing the absence of food in the room guided them away from these selections.

Once a song was initiated, it was critical to carefully monitor the child's reaction. By positioning themselves close enough to make eye contact, but not so close as to be upsetting, they were able to observe facial expressions and body language. Having all songs committed to memory allowed Jim and Paul to observe how the child was responding to the music. Paying undivided attention to the child, scanning for signs of positive or negative feedback and adjusting accordingly, emerged as a key element of the TME discipline.

Despite their improving ability to make appropriate song choices, on occasion a child would become disturbed by their music. Jim and Paul developed an exit strategy where they would continue playing as they backed out of the room into the hallway. It was a way of acknowledgingthe feedback and honoring the child without abandoning their belief that the music, if given due time, would be helpful.

Jim recalled how he made inaccurate song selections when he first started visiting hospitals. "I would decide to do something up-tempo and immediately the child would be overwhelmed. At first, I would just apologize and leave the room. Later on, I got more comfortable transitioning to a different song or continuing with the same song but lightening it up a bit to give the child some distance until they stopped crying or whimpering. I had to have all of those experiences to figure out how to read the signals better. It was a major learning curve."

The first few times Jim played for a sick child he didn't perceive much of a response. He recalled one day when he played for three or four children in the hospital playroom while they sat emotionless throughout the entire twenty-minute session. He wondered, *Why did I even bother to do this?*

But the nurse came up to him afterward and said, "This was wonderful."

"It was?" asked Jim.

"Yes. One little boy hadn't been out of his room for about five weeks. He heard the music and came down the hall."

Sometimes a child's signs of engagement with the music appeared in more subtle ways, such as a peek over the sheets, a slight smile, or the covert tapping of the foot under the covers of an otherwise expressionless child. Once he had learned how to read the signs, Jim found that the response was almost always there. When it was not visible, Jim discovered that the impact might not occur until long after he had left the room and the messages and experience of the song were given time to settle into the child's mind and heart.

There was also the challenge of how to best bid farewell to the audience. Jim and Paul learned that while it was tempting to say, "I hope you get better," or "I hope you feel better," those comments implied the promise of a cure they could not guarantee. "I put my foot in my mouth many times going out the door," said Jim. "One kind child life specialist told me to never say, 'I hope you get to go home soon,' because they may not get well and go home." Based on that feedback, Jim developed a fairly standard farewell that was encouraging and optimistic without providing false hope: "I hope you have a wonderful today and an even better tomorrow."

Because Jim and Paul had entertained for many years, they realized that in the hospital the relationship between audience and performer needed reconsideration. While many of the skills they honed through years of performing proved helpful, in the hospital they had to consider themselves as servant musicians. They learned to concentrate on the music as an aid to healing, not an end in itself. Attention was directed at the patient and to other family members present, not at the musician. Success would not be defined by how well the song was performed but by how well it was received.

The duration of each individual room visit is brief, perhaps five minutes in length—enough time for Jim and Paul to introduce themselves, make sure music is desired, play a song, and bid farewell. These brief encounters of caring and support required something from Jim and Paul that could not be taught. It was a dimension found deep within that might best be described as an authentic presence that derives from the fact they care enough about children they don't know to be with them for a few minutes and try to make their day a better one. According to Renee Hunte, Program Manager for Child and Adolescent Life at Duke University Hospital:

> **The thing I love the most about Jim and Paul is their presence. I appreciate what they bring to families, not only their gift of song but also their ability to relate to patients. Their demeanor in the hospital environment is very calm, relaxed, and engaging. It's never about them. It's always about that patient.**

Describing how unique KidLinks TME is in the world of child life resources, Chris Brown, child life director at Hassenfeld Children's Hospital at NYU Langone Medical Center, said, "As far as I know, there are no other entities out there like KidLinks, specifically looking at what the needs of these kids are and finding ways to respond through music to them. There aren't others writing their own music and going into hospitals to personally interact with the kids." In a similar vein, Jim would later say, "I think we have created a discipline, this manner of doing music that is a lot more than just doing music."

This unique and effective blend of dedicated song and service increased demand for Jim's and Paul's TME visits. From 1995 to 2004, they averaged over 150 days each year, providing music in hospitals and at camps that served children, teens, and families impacted by a chronic illness. In addition, they spent an additional two to three weeks each year recording new songs or attending conferences, sharing their discipline and establishing new contacts.

Being away from the office for three-fourths of their workdays resulted in the need for someone to run the home base when Jim and Paul were on the road. For more than a decade, that responsibility fell on a part-time administrative assistant who handled correspondence, kept records, and made travel arrangements for Jim and Paul. While Karen Murphy's official title may have included the word "assistant," according to Paul, "Karen *was* the administrator. She did pretty much everything we needed done."

Karen's work was so critical that Paul bestowed her with the moniker "Mothership" because she served as command headquarters when Jim and Paul were traveling. In a time when there were no cell phones, Paul recalls, "We would stop at pay phones so that Jim would call Karen to see what was going on, or to have her communicate with our next stop, or change our motel reservation. She was our lifeline as we journeyed around the country playing various hospitals and camps."

Karen described her time supporting the duo in equally positive terms. "Working for Celebration Shop [later Hugworks] was one of the highlights of my working experiences," she said. "I totally believed in the cause and saw for myself the positive effect their music had on children and families. It was a blessing to be part of something that changed lives and brought comfort to so many!"

According to Paul, "Karen was by far the most dedicated, committed employee in the history of the organization." Jim echoed that sentiment.

"Karen's support during those eleven years made each day of our service possible. We could not have done our work without her."

CHAPTER NINE

A Day in the Life

On numerous occasions, Jim would spend the night sleeping in their office building in the Dallas–Fort Worth (DFW) mid-cities suburb of Hurst. His home was almost an hour drive to the south; since he needed to be at Children's Medical Center near downtown Dallas by nine the next morning, sleeping on the office cot allowed him to cut the commute though Metroplex traffic that by 2012 had become increasingly congested. This also freed him to dedicate a couple of extra hours behind the desk instead of the wheel. The downside of an overnight stay in the office was Jim's inability to escape the demands of the enterprise he had founded. The number of items on his to-do list grew constantly: finishing the donor newsletter, reviewing the general ledger, and contacting out-of-state hospitals regarding possible future visits.

Entering Jim's office space was like stepping into a three-dimensional scrapbook of his life and career. A large, framed poster of John Denver dominated one corner, while certificates from numerous awards were neatly organized along the adjoining wall. On the corner of Jim's desk stood a yellow and white neon light shaped like the silhouette of a palm tree wearing a halo that Jim called the Holy Palm. On its base was taped a small scrap of paper, there for Jim to read every day. For over twenty years, the note served as a reminder of why he started Hugworks. "It was so simple," he told his visitor. "I don't recall the hospital. This little boy looked too young to even be writing." The note, scribbled in pencil on a little torn piece of paper,

I think [*sic*] you for what you did Jim.
I know that it is true.

"For years, I carried it around in my guitar case everywhere I went to preserve it." It was a cherished compliment from one of those he had come to admire and trust—a little child facing significant life challenges.

Jim cherished the life lessons children taught him over the years. At summer camps for children with cancer, he marveled at a level of maturity that belied their ages. Because of what they had suffered, most demonstrated an older person's wisdom in a young child's body. "I think kids who have been or are at risk, whether that has been a medical or an emotional risk, are more in touch with their feelings because they've had to be. They feel more deeply, too. Things just connect with them at a deeper level," Jim explained.

One year at camp, Jim had been watching the kids play baseball when a young boy going through chemo approached him. The eleven-year-old had lost most of his hair and looked emaciated. After saying hello they sat in silence for a few minutes until the child spoke again.

"You know I am going to die, don't you?" he had said, without looking Jim's direction.

"Are you?" Jim had asked, uncertain where their conversation was headed.

"Yes, I am. But you can't tell my mom and dad because they can't handle it."

"How do you feel about dying?"

"I am ready for it. I am tired and I don't want to hurt anymore. I don't want to have this chemo anymore. I know I am going to be with God and I'm gonna be fine."

The conversation epitomized what Jim admired about these children—their resilience, inherent spirituality, and readiness to talk about issues that adults might avoid. "Kids are so authentic," said Jim. "Kids tell you exactly how they feel until we train them not to anymore."

*****

Jolted back into the moment, Jim realized he needed to leave the office soon. But of immediate concern was the location of one of his letter-sized yellow notepads. He was pretty sure, although far from certain, that it was hiding somewhere in his office. He rifled through stacks of items scattered across the floor and tabletops—anywhere there was a flat surface. Because Jim kept almost every item he touched, one might assume that he had an effective filing system. He did. Unfortunately, he lacked an adequate file retrieval system, and this missing yellow writing tablet was merely the latest casualty.

The yellow pads were vital to Jim because they contained notes and reminders that helped him keep track of everything that needed to be done, which was a lot. The notes couldn't be called "to-do lists" because that would imply some logic or structure. These notepads resembled patchwork quilts of blue ink graffiti sewn onto a yellow background. Scribbles populated entire pages. Some followed the printed lines while others were written at odd and oblique angles. Some groups of words were circled; others were lined through. A few entries had arrows or stars next to them, suggesting that some heightened sense of urgency applied to them. Only Jim knew what all these symbols meant.

To avoid being late, Jim decided to abandon the notepad search, trusting it would show up later. That's how it usually turned out. *It might even be in my rolling office parked around back of the building*, Jim thought.

Jim hopped in his company car and, after making a brief visit at a nearby 7-Eleven to grab a Diet Coke, began his trek toward the hospital near downtown Dallas. With each occasional sip out of his Big Gulp cup, Jim hoped for a surge in psychic energy that would ready him for a visit to a hospital he had visited hundreds of times to sing songs he had sung for over a quarter century.

The trip to the hospital was a breeze, as Jim encountered none of the traffic snarls that had come to plague Dallas-area commuters. After wheeling into the Green Lot where volunteers were directed to park, he donned his red shirt with an embroidered logo, grabbed his guitar, and began the long journey to the volunteers' office where he checked in and met Paul, who had arrived a few minutes earlier.

The morning went well as Jim and Paul roamed the outpatient waiting rooms in search of opportunities to create "flash concerts" for the children and family members seated there. This activity took about two hours, so by noon, a break provided them an hour to eat lunch, chat, return phone calls, and prepare for visits to individual patient rooms starting at one o'clock.

On this day, Paul had an afternoon conflict, so Jim planned to handle the room visits on his own. As he strolled down the hall of the unit with his guitar strapped over his shoulder, Jim seemed out of place in this sterile hospital environment. He paused outside a room to study the small piece of paper listing the room numbers of patients whom the staff in the Child Life Department suggested might benefit from a visit.

Certain he was at the right room, he tapped on the door three times with his knuckles—loud enough to announce his presence but not so loud as to disrupt whatever rest might be taking place on the other side. He cracked the door open and peeked inside. Noting that the ten-year-old girl and her mother were both awake, he opened the door a bit wider and entered. "Hello. My name is Jim. The child life folks said you might like a song."

The question surprised mother and child. Hospitals don't offer many choices, particularly a request like this one. The girl sat up in bed and smiled, signaling to Jim that she was open to the idea. The mother seemed even more positive, something Jim often found with parents. She may have needed a distraction, some new source of energy, to break the monotony of the bedside vigil. The mother looked at her daughter for any indication of rejection on her part. Seeing none, she said, "Yes, a song would be nice."

Jim studied the child to make sure she was comfortable with her mom's decision. If the girl showed any hint of reservation in her voice or body language, he would thank them both and leave. Jim had learned that giving kids a chance to say no in this environment could be a better gift than a song.

Having gained permission, Jim's attention turned to the next challenge: finding the right song to fit the moment. In an environment filled with the sights and sounds of the latest medical technology, he relied on years of experience and thousands of room visits like this one to guide his decision. He scanned the room for clues. The shades were open and the room was bright, indicating something with a bit of energy would fit the environment. Since mother and child were both present, a song that engaged them equally would be ideal. Jim cross-referenced these inputs against the list of songs in his mental repertoire and arrived at his choice.

Jim positioned himself close enough to establish eye contact with the girl but not so close that his large frame would seem threatening. He kept the mother in his line of sight, but her daughter had the front-row seat for this concert. He looked directly at the girl and introduced his song with a smile and a soothing baritone voice: "This song tells you that the only thing you have to do to be your best . . . is just be *you*."

The rich, twelve-string resonance of his Guild guitar filled the room, soon joined by Jim's molasses-smooth baritone voice:

I can't stand on a distant planet
I can't stand on my sister Janet
I can't stand on a rhino's snout
I can't stand brussels sprouts

A smile crossed the faces of both daughter and mother. Such silly words! Little did they know that the humor of the verse is there to grab their attention and prepare them for the exhortation of encouragement reflected in the chorus:

But I can be the best I can be
I can be the best I can be
Take a look at me and you'll see
I can be the best I can be
I can do the best I can do
I can do the best I can do
And I'm gonna bet you can, too
You can do the best you can do

Mother and daughter were both smiling, a sign they were engaged in the music and the moment. They swapped smiles and gazed back at Jim, who winked at the girl as he began the second verse:

I can't drive a circus train
I can't drive a big jet airplane
I can't drive my dad to work
But sometimes I drive Mom berserk

Both laughed at the honest human truth of the lyrics. Yes, they did occasionally get on each other's nerves, but this was neither the time nor the place to dwell on that. It was time to share a positive moment together. Jim's song gave them something to smile about and reminded them how much they needed each other.

Jim finished the song and smiled at the little girl. Her contemplative look signaled to him that she was processing the song's message, reflecting on what it meant for her.

"That was wonderful," said the mom, as she clapped her hands. Her daughter followed suit. Through years of experience, Jim knew that the children look to their parents for cues. When the parents responded to the music, whether that response was in the form of a laugh, a smile, a clap, or a tear, it gave the child permission to express his or her feelings. It worked in the other direction, too, when the children took the lead.

"Let's all give your best a big round of applause," Jim said, deflecting attention back to the girl.

As he turned to leave, Jim reached into his shirt pocket and gave the little girl a card that served as a tangible reminder of their visit and contained useful tips on how to use music and song to help children. "I hope you have a great today and an even better tomorrow. And I hope you always keep a song in your heart," said Jim. "It will make a big difference in how you feel . . . and how you heal."

His wording was intentional. Jim could not promise a *cure*. Neither could the doctors, nurses, or her mother. It would be a mistake to think "healing" and "curing" are the same thing. They differ both in terms of approach and what is demanded. "Curing" focuses on fixing, correcting, or rectifying specific physical ailments. But "healing" concentrates on making the entire person whole by addressing matters of the soul, spirit, and mind regardless of medical outcome. This process of helping those who suffer become whole is central to Jim's understanding of the world and his role as servant in it.

As Jim exited their room, he left it a better place than when he had arrived only five minutes earlier. He now felt a renewed sense of inner energy. Giving the gift of his music to those who need it always lifted his spirits, no matter how he felt when he entered the hospital to sing. "I can't remember a time I ever came away from the hospital wishing I hadn't gone that day," said Jim. "There have been plenty of days when I didn't want to go. As I get older there are more of those than there used to be. I just have less energy, less 'spizorinctum'—as my dad would call it—less get-upand-go. But I still get so much from seeing people lifted by our music that I am being lifted, too. It changes my mood. It helps me heal my inner child."

The music served Jim as he served others.

Back in the hallway, Jim pulled the small sheet of paper back out of his pocket to find the next room on the list. *Good*, he thought to himself. *It's just a couple of doors down.* He tapped on the door three times—loud enough to announce his presence but not so loud that it might disrupt whatever rest might be taking place on the other side. He opened the door slowly and peeked inside. Noting a father and his son awake inside, Jim pushed the door open widely and said, "Hello. My name is Jim. The child life folks said you might like a song."

THE ORGANIZATION

CHAPTER TEN

A Rose by a Different Name

Jim Newton founded Celebration Shop in 1981 as a 501(c)(3) personal ministry focused toward youth and young adults. He combined a unique blend of Scripture, singing, and storytelling to illustrate a wide range of themes—for example,

- "God Made Me (and God Don't Make No Junk)"—A *celebration* of God's special creation in *you*!

- "Every Time I Find Out Where It's at Somebody Moves It"—An affirmation that God is with us even in our pain and failure.

- "Rock-a-Bye Sweet Starchild"—A *celebration* of the Starchild within us all.

The word "celebration" appeared numerous times in the promotional materials Jim created. He interpreted the word more broadly than its typical association with festivities associated with a noteworthy occasion. "I always loved the concept of celebrating all that life had to offer—the good and the bad, the highs and the lows," said Jim. His personal connection to the word was strong, reflected in the notes he routinely sent to supporters, which closed with "In Celebration."

When Jim was looking for a word to complement "celebration," he found an instructive model in PBS's Children's Television Workshop, which began producing educational programs—most notably *Sesame*

Street—in 1970. Jim liked the placeness, the quality of coming from some physical location, that "workshop" conveyed for their brand. Jim felt the combination of "celebration" and "shop" captured the essence of what he hoped his nonprofit could provide: a space where celebrations were created.

Jim felt the Celebration Shop name continued to work as the focus of his mission shifted in the mid-1980s to severely ill children and their caregivers. But by the year 2000, Jim had grown weary of the pervasive confusion associated with it. People struggled to remember the name correctly, with new and incorrect variations appearing on a regular basis: Celebration Workshop, Celebrity Shop, Celebration Station. "Folks kept finding new ways to get it wrong," said Jim. After twenty years of having to correct them, Jim took the hint. It was time for a change.

*****

In June 2004, Celebration Shop board members and staff participated in a workshop to address the ongoing confusion regarding the organization's name. Their initial task was to develop a list of attributes that distinguished Celebration Shop from other nonprofit enterprises. Attendees were asked to respond to this question: what, if anything, makes Celebration Shop unique? Following an extended discussion, they aligned on this description dated June 12, 2004:

> **Others may sing in clinical settings (with varying degrees of professionalism and altruism). And others may write positive music for children. Others may have a passion and sensitivity for children and their caregivers. But it is through a unique combination of these elements that Celebration Shop has approached its work which makes it truly unique.**

The meeting surfaced many suggestions for a new name for the organization, but none struck the group as an improvement. Finally, one participant said, "What about the name for our album series— Hugworks? We like it for that, so why not call the organization Hugworks?" Everyone loved the idea and agreed that it accurately captured their mission. The organization started operating under the new name in the middle of 2004.[1]

The Hugworks name initially emerged in conjunction with work on the team's second album, *We Can Do*. After one of Jim's supporters presented to him a possible cover design, Jim thought it would be wise to show the rendering to his friend David Michel. David and his wife had developed a successful animated television series called *Jay Jay the Jet Plane* that followed the adventures of a curious six-year-old jet airplane who lived at an airport "where imagination takes flight!" David told Jim that he didn't think the new design was engaging enough to capture attention and recommended that Jim contact the creative design agency that helped him find the right look for the Jay Jay character and his friends.

Jim brought his guitar to the initial meeting with Mark Sullivan, cofounder of the Sullivan Herndon agency.[2] After hearing Jim tell his story and sing a couple of songs, Mark was hooked. "I felt the goodliness, the godliness, in what he was doing," said Mark. "You could just tell by the look in his eyes that Jim was a legitimate guy who believed through and through that the children needed to hear his music to get through rough times."

The agency accepted the assignment to create graphics for the *We Can Do* album release. Since Jim and Paul were also planning to reissue their first album, originally called *Friends of the Family*, under the new title *Best I Can Be*, Sullivan Herndon recommended they promote the two albums as a series with a consistent look and name. After gaining approval, the agency assessed Celebration Shop's music and service from a new perspective. "We tried to define what their music did when played to children," said Mark. "We thought it was like their songs

---

1   In an ironic twist, the Hugworks name encountered a fate similar to that of Celebration Shop. With the publication of J. K. Rowling's *Harry Potter* series, "Hogwarts" sunk roots deep in the pop culture lexicon. The name referred to the Hogwarts School of Witchcraft and Wizardry, a fictional boarding school of magic that served as the main setting for the first six Harry Potter books released between 1997 and 2005. Due to their immense popularity—the series sold more than five hundred million copies—the Hogwarts name became so seeded into the consciousness of young and old readers that there was no way any organization, much less a small nonprofit, could compete with such a close-sounding one.

2   Sullivan Herndon now operates under the name Character Farms. According to Mark Sullivan, Character Farms began in 2008 after a project to retheme a friend's new dental office. Mark soon realized his true calling was to create fun and engaging themed environments for children. He shared his vision with his best friend and notable illustrator Ernest "Ernie" Pacheco, and soon thereafter Character Farms was born. For more information, visit www.characterfarms.com.

were hugging the children at a time when they needed to be hugged. There were a lot of brand names around that time that came out with the word 'works' as part of it, so we figured that's what they do. They manufacture hugs for children through the music. That's how we came up with Hugworks."

Mark's agency developed a lighthearted way of portraying the Hugworks brand through cartoonlike characters. Some of these—a fish, a frog, and a bee—were mentioned in songs on the albums. Other characters were also developed, although what genus or species they may represent is not clear. Lower-case letters were used throughout to project a friendly and approachable look and feel. These graphic elements were included in all three albums of the "Hugworks Series" initially launched with *We Can Do* and *Best I Can Be* in 1998, followed by *World around Song* in 2002.

*****

The branding workshop produced something more valuable than a new name for the organization. By articulating the elements that uniquely defined its mission, the Hugworks team established a blueprint that could guide future initiatives. This brand polestar was initially expressed as a formula consisting of these elements:

High product quality. Jim's intent from day one was that the work his nonprofit produced must be of the highest possible quality. He established the benchmark to be "good enough to compete with Disney." With Noel "Paul" Stookey on the team with Jim and Paul, their award-winning recordings met or exceeded that lofty goal. In addition, the team asserted everything done by the organization needed to meet a . . .

Professional performance level. Jim considered singing for the children in the hospital a service, not a performance. But a professional level of delivery was required for the messages contained in the songs to get through without distraction. These messages were important because they were based on an understanding of . . .

Audience needs translated into the songwriting process. Perhaps the clearest distinction between Jim's, Paul's, and Noel's songs compared to other children's music was the degree to which they were intentionally composed and later subjected to the review of experts to ensure they contained helpful messages. Despite this self-imposed constraint, they were able to create an impressive repertoire of carefully crafted songs that spoke to a wide range of needs and offered help and healing. But sharing these songs in hospitals demanded . . .

Sensitivity to persons and issues in the client setting. Jim and Paul learned that singing in clinical settings involved much more than musical skills. Effectiveness depended on the ability to read the situation, determine whether the child wanted a song, make an appropriate selection, not hinder the work of medical staff, and more. Providing music in hospitals required a level of sensitivity to the environment and the people that many musicians may not naturally have. Over time, Jim's and Paul's service translated into . . .

Proven experience in the field. In its first twenty years of existence, Celebration Shop brought therapeutic music to tens of thousands of children and their caregivers. Jim and Paul's commitment and consistent caring provided the organization with an unmatched level of credibility that can only come through experience.

Gaining clarity regarding what made its mission unique was an important step forward for the Hugworks team. The ability to articulate how your work is one-of-a-kind is critical for any brand but particularly for nonprofit organizations where the mission drives emotional and financial support that sustains programs. The final report from the branding workshop evokes the overused Shakespeare quote that suggests what you name something is less important than what you do. "All agreed that the name change is only that—the essence of Hugworks is well-defined, unchanged, and still vitally important to all connected with the organization."

CHAPTER ELEVEN

It Takes a Few Angels

Raising funds to support their programs is the greatest challenge all nonprofits face—one that never goes away. "Nonprofit" is a tax status, not a guarantee of financial security. While a charitable organization may be passionate about its mission, financial viability requires constant fundraising and budgetary management. According to some experts, this means that to be successful, as Tracy Ebarb wrote in "Nonprofits Fail: Here's Seven Reasons Why" for the NANOE blog, "Nonprofits need to place their donors as their top priority because without them there would be no impact—no people served, no mouths fed, no backs clothed."

Celebration Shop was no different. From the beginning, funding was the biggest obstacle that stood in the way of Jim's transition into his new mission. Jim needed to replace the money he had earned through honoraria from his youth work with funds from donors. Despite the challenges, the encouragement Jim received from others kept him going. He cannot recall who said it, but a message from one early supporter stuck with Jim: "What you are doing is such a good thing that I know some angels will come along and help you out. Just be patient."

"Angels" great and small visited Jim in time, but only after years of hard work drumming up the grassroots support that is the lifeblood of most charitable causes. Each December, Jim sent letters to donors on his mailing list containing a personal, handwritten note. "I would receive small gifts of about $10 to $25 from three hundred or so of these," said Jim. "In the early days of Celebration Shop, the bulk of our funds came from small donors."

On occasion, Jim would receive a more substantial gift, like one from a couple who sent a check for $10,000 with a note reading, "We love what you are doing." There was also a donation from a retired woman who heard Jim sing at a nearby United Methodist church and sent him a check for $20,000. Longtime friend and banker Grant Hollingsworth offered financial support whenever a little extra came his way, like the year he gave part of his annual bonus to support Celebration Shop programs. "We loved receiving major gifts, but we relied on regular donors who gave each year to keep going," said Jim.

One of Jim's most consistent supporters was Dallas energy businessman J. W. Brown, who first met Jim at Highland Park United Methodist Church located adjacent to the SMU campus. In the late 1980s, J.W. and his wife, Ann, started attending a young adult Bible study along with about twenty other couples. Jim, who had graduated from SMU's Perkins School of Theology, visited one of the sessions and shared a few of his songs. "I thought it was pretty cool," J.W. recalls. "We bought a couple of his original cassette tapes, and when one of our girls got sick, we would pop one into the player and let them listen. They really liked it. We would play it for them in the car when we would go on road trips." According to Jim,

J.W. and his wife became regular donors during the first few years after they met. "He would send a number of checks in growing amounts each year, which was a pretty big deal for us."

The trajectory of J.W.'s career stands in striking contrast to that of Jim, who shifted from attending seminary, to playing with the Pilgrimage Band in bars and honkytonks, and then to his ministry with youth. Meanwhile, J.W. brought a laser focus to his career. After graduating from law school at SMU, he moved to Tulsa where he was a practicing attorney for two years. Following his marriage, J.W. moved back to Dallas to work as in-house counsel for an energy company and then later set up a small oil and gas company with a friend. "I really wanted to get after it!" he said.

A couple years later, oil prices had dropped to a low $8 a barrel, forcing J.W. to search for funding sources. J.W. read an article about an investment banker in Denver who was putting together capital for oil and gas companies. "I called him to see if he could help me raise money and during our conversation, he told me he wanted to open an office in Dallas and I could fill that role if I was interested. So I dissolved our company and became an energy investment banker."

J.W.'s timing was unfortunate as a significant downturn was occurring in the industry in the late 1980s. But J.W. found opportunity amid the decline. "The small guys didn't have anywhere to go for funding, so there was a vacuum. I traveled to towns where the bigger investors wouldn't go. I made a good business out of focusing on the independents for the next twenty-five years. I also made a lot of contacts along the way."

✶✶✶✶✶

A book J.W. read shortly after its release in 1994 moved him to do more for Jim and Celebration Shop. *Halftime: Moving from Success to Significance* delivered a message at a time when J.W. was ready to receive it. Written by Christian businessman Bob Buford, *Halftime* suggests that midlife should not be considered a time of crisis but rather an opportunity to dedicate one's self toward pursuing a lasting legacy.

According to Buford, during the first part of our lives most of us are focused on self, family, and career—what he calls "achieving, gaining, learning, earning." But in the "second half," Buford suggests that a reorientation toward using the talents and resources we have been blessed with to serve others will make one's second half better than the first.

Buford's message forced J.W. to reconsider his direction in life. Like so many professionals who worked hard and achieved success, J.W. wondered what he may have missed along the way. "It got me thinking about what I wanted to be remembered for. I didn't know what the answer was, but I was pretty sure it wasn't that I had made a good living in the energy business."

Half Time provided the nudge J.W. needed to seek out second-half significance in his life. Not long after reading it, he started looking for something that would leverage the talents and numerous business contacts he had developed during his career. His devotion to the underdogs in this world, like the small energy guys he helped earlier as a banker, made Jim and Celebration Shop a perfect fit. But most of all, going into the hospital and seeing the impact for himself forged his empathy for the cause. "I got hooked early on with what Jim did with the kids," said J.W. "I could see it time and again as I went into hospitals. I developed a real belief that a lot of good things come out of it. I guess everybody needs a focus and a mission. This one is mine."

By the mid-1990s, Jim and Paul were preparing to record their second album, *We Can Do*. After the songs had been written and reviewed by the advisory panel, Jim sent a letter to major donors asking for funds for the recording session. Upon seeing the request, J.W. convinced the Dallas Energy Finance Discussion Group, which he had helped start a few years earlier, to donate $30,000 to the effort, to which he added his own personal contribution of $5,000. "We could have never done that album without J.W.'s help," recalls Jim.

J.W. and Jim's relationship grew with time. Whenever Jim encountered a problem he was unsure how to handle, J.W. was at the top of his list of people to call. That was the case in 2005 when the opportunity to purchase an office building fell into Jim's lap. He had been working free of charge out of space at the First United Methodist Church in Hurst, Texas. In return, Jim provided programs for the congregation's youth and music during worship services. The church owned a nearby building that housed Mission Central, which included a food pantry and clothing bank. When that mission outgrew the space and moved down the street, church leaders approached Jim and asked him if he wanted to buy the building for what they had paid for it a few years earlier, far below its market value.

The idea of housing his nonprofit in an office building had never crossed Jim's mind, and the deal seemed too good to be true. Jim approached J.W. and asked for his advice. "You'd be a fool not to buy it," said J.W. "But just to make sure, I'll provide $5,000 to conduct a feasibility study to do the necessary inspections to make sure there are no issues." Celebration Shop bought the building and moved in three months later.

For years, a glazed wooden plaque hung near the front entrance to the Hugworks office. Dated September 2008, it acknowledged organizations and individuals who had provided significant financial support for the mission. The plaque served as a constant reminder to Jim that he could not have kept his mission going without the help of countless others.

The second line of the inscription honored "An Anonymous Christian Energy Industry Businessman." J.W. had introduced the man to Jim after the man had voiced concern over the absence of overt Christian messages in the songs Jim and Paul were singing to severely ill children in the hospital. He believed Jim was missing out on an opportunity to spread the gospel to those suffering and in need. He shared his concern with J.W., who told him, "Let's go talk to Jim about it."

After hearing him out, Jim said to the businessman, "The hospitals won't let us do religious songs, so we couldn't if we wanted. But I am not going to hide behind that because I think we need to respect where people are in their faith journey. What we do is translate the gospel message of love into songs that everyone can hear. I think there is a place for that. That is my ministry and my mission."

Jim then invited the gentleman to join him on one of his upcoming hospital visits. "Come see for yourself," Jim had told him. He accepted the offer and afterward told Jim and Paul, "Well, I still wish you guys could use Christian language, but I think I understand a bit better now."

A few months later, J.W. Brown invited Jim to lunch with that same businessman. After they had been seated, J.W. said, "Jim, I think you are going to be happy because at one o'clock this afternoon a wire transfer for $100,000 is going to the bank to pay off the mortgage [$78,000] on your building. Plus, the extra funds above the mortgage payoff will help you with some of your other projects."

"Wow!" Jim responded. "Who in the world would do that?"

"The guy wants to remain anonymous to others, but he is sitting to your right."

Then the donor told Jim, "I really believe in you and what you are doing and I wanted to help. I just sold my company and can afford to give some money away, so I decided to pay your building off."

*****

The energy industry has experienced more than its share of ups and downs over the years, not only in terms of profits but also public distrust. In the late 1990s, business was robust but consumers were protesting the substantial amounts of money oil and gas companies were making. "We were considered the bad guys at the time," J.W. reflects. "I remember thinking there must be something we could do to give energy guys a little more positive exposure . . . an event that was fun but also gave back to the community." Recalling discussions with Jim about his need for money to finish a number of projects, J.W. made a connection. "I thought, *Maybe there is a way to improve perceptions of the energy business and help out Jim at the same time.*"

With the help of four other energy businessmen, J.W. decided to hold a golf tournament. "There were a lot of these where you basically go play golf, drink beer, and meet other people. They were just social events. There was no cause that was helped as a result." J.W. suggested that Celebration Shop might be a charity everyone could support. He took the group to the hospital to see Jim and Paul in action, and once they saw them sing to the children, the group of businessmen agreed to support the idea.

Before the tournament, J.W. told anyone who would listen how this was going to be much more than a social event. But when he mentioned Celebration Shop as the cause being supported, many would say, "What is that? I never heard of that." While J.W. would try to explain, he learned quickly that the story "just wasn't sticky enough for people to identify with." To address this messaging challenge, two local hospitals that Jim and Paul were visiting each month—Cook Children's in Fort Worth and Children's Medical Center in Dallas—were added as beneficiaries. By packaging Celebration Shop with two known and respected entities, J.W. was able to simultaneously enhance the event's fundraising potential and elevate Celebration Shop as a viable charity.

In preparation for the golf tournament, a nonprofit foundation was created with 501(c)(3) status. When J.W. realized they were missing a name for the event, he asked Jim for help. Jim conducted his own personal brainstorming session. "Let's see. This will benefit children, so maybe 'kid' needs to be in the name. And it involves golf, so maybe 'links' will work. How about KidLinks?" After J.W. endorsed the name, Jim enlisted his son, Jeremy, to create a visual image to express it. Jeremy produced a stick figure of a golfer wearing his hat backward and preparing to swing a golf club. Striking in its simplicity, the image continues to be the logo for the event more than twenty years later.

The inaugural KidLinks Energy Golf Classic took place in the fall of 2001. About one hundred people attended that day, including Noel "Paul" Stookey, who greeted each golfer at the tee box of one of the par-3s. Before they teed off, every player had their picture taken with the celebrity. Net proceeds from this first event totaled around $100,000, half of which went to Celebration Shop and the other half to the hospitals. The success provided the newly formed KidLinks Foundation with encouragement to repeat the event. Over the next two years, the event grew dramatically in terms of attendance, cost, and complexity, so an executive director was hired to plan it. Entertainment the night before the golf outing was added, including performances by Texas music celebrities Clint Black and Pat Green in different years.

J.W. was not a fan of the emerging business model for the event, nor the optics associated with it. "I got real bothered about how much money we were spending. We had more money coming in but we were giving the same amount of money to the charities as were back before we did all of that extra stuff. We were spending money on a party that should be going to the children in the hospital," said J.W. "Plus, the big party was reinforcing the bad-guy image for the energy business."

Two distinct factions formed inside the KidLinks board, and feuding and fighting began over the future direction for the event. One side advocated the bigger-is-better approach that emulated a highbrow social event which received significant exposure, like the annual Cattle Baron's Ball in Dallas. J.W. pushed for a modest yet high-quality approach that combined lower costs with growing the number of attendees as the formula for raising more money for the charities. During one board meeting, material disagreement arose over which path to take going forward. In the end, J.W.'s approach prevailed, and four members resigned from the board.

Set on the course that is still in place today, the KidLinks Energy Golf Classic has established a solid reputation as an event that meets J.W.'s original concept. "It works great. Everybody has a good time," said J.W. "We have the model and have been very careful not to tinker with it. You know, if it's not broke, don't fix it."

The success of the golf event served as prologue for J.W. He searched for an additional event that could attract a different audience from golfers. The fruit of that effort was the KidLinks Symphony of Chefs, which first took place in the winter of 2011. It is an interactive culinary experience where guests enjoy a chef-prepared, four-course dinner with wine pairings from some of the world's best vineyards. "While the costs associated with this event are higher, it generates a nice income," J.W. explained.

Over the past twenty years, the KidLinks Energy Golf Classic and Symphony of Chefs have raised nearly $5 million in support of programs dedicated to addressing the plight of severely ill children. Today, all proceeds are directed toward Jim's mission because J.W.'s efforts made it a known entity among the Texas energy business community. According to Jim, "I don't think we would have made it without J.W. Maybe some other angel would have come along, but I doubt they would have been as generous or committed. He and his wife gave us a lot of money over the years, but he did more than that. J.W. gifted us with his personal reputation. He introduced us to many other people who believed in us because they believed in him."

CHAPTER TWELVE

Reaching a Breaking Point

As 2012 drew to a close, Jim Newton was feeling good about the direction of Hugworks. The next year would be the start of his fourth decade of bringing the healing power of music to kids who needed to hear it most. Even better, Jim had been freed from growing administrative duties with the hiring of a full-time executive director twelve months earlier. He could now focus on what had fueled his passion for so many years: bringing his songs to children and their caregivers in hospitals, camps, and special care facilities.

The creation of the separate executive director position was a no-brainer for Jim. Part of this understanding came from his board of directors, who suggested it was time for someone else to handle the managerial duties. Aware of his administrative deficiencies, Jim had reached the same conclusion months earlier. "I was worn out from thirty years of trying to be all things to all people—raise money, plan events, write and record songs, and provide direct service," said Jim. "I was probably a fairly good administrator for a musician, but that was no longer good enough given the way we had grown."

The change in leadership was contributing to progress on a number of programmatic fronts. Having a full-time director responsible for running Hugworks allowed Jim to spend more time visiting hospitals. The number of children and parents served though in-person therapeutic music entertainment sessions had grown more than 11 percent in 2012 over the prior year. New songs had been identified, with a recording session planned in May 2013 that would include Noel and some of the best studio musicians available. Plans were in place to expand free music therapy sessions conducted by board-certified practitioners and subsidized by Hugworks. "Life was good," said Jim.

But just as the program side of the nonprofit work was moving at a quickened pace, the Hugworks train started to derail with the executive director's resignation. Jim had no way of knowing that, in the months ahead, Hugworks would head into a season of bitter darkness that jeopardized everything he had worked so hard and so long to create.

*****

Work was piling up in early 2013 as Jim found himself back at the Hugworks helm. While he was not formally given the title of acting executive director until six months later, Jim filled the managerial vacuum because "the work had to be done and I was the only one there to do it." The list of things to do on Jim's yellow notepads grew longer, with fewer items being crossed off each day. The frequent meetings, communications to donors, and budget management were all pulling him away from hospital visits. Then, a couple months after returning to his old role, Hugworks' business manager also resigned, leaving him with more work and stress. "I picked up again because I had to. But I was burned out—big time," said Jim. It was about to get worse.

On the morning of March 25, 2013, Jim headed to the office a little earlier than usual. It would be the first full day on the job for a temporary business manager and Jim wanted to be there to help her gain her bearings. It turned out she was a quick study. "Mr. Newton," she said when Jim walked in. "I think you better sit down because I have something bad to share with you. You have had money fraudulently taken from your account, maybe as much as $90,000."

"What?"

"Your prior business manager has been fraudulently using a company credit card, and the executive director was not paying attention to what was going on," she said.

As they pored over the details together, it became clear the previous business manager had been padding expense reports and pocketing cash through bogus credit card charges. Her supervisor had not been reviewing the general ledger during her thirteen months on the job, nor had she scrutinized credit card bill details before signing payment vouchers. Jim fumed over the ugly irony of it all: If a temporary employee was able to discover the theft during her first couple hours on the job, the problem should have been obvious all along. When a full accounting was complete, the amount stolen totaled $93,000.

Reputation may be the most precious asset any nonprofit possesses, and Jim was furious that people he trusted had put at risk the goodwill that had taken him three decades to build. Worried about the damage this might have on relationships with those who supported him, Jim made calls to major donors and members of his board to tell them the discovery and to apologize. "They needed to hear it from me," Jim said. "I was confident they wouldn't blame me because it had not been my responsibility, but I was afraid they might kill the messenger."

According to Jim, "Everyone was wonderful." True to form, J.W. offered perspective and advice that extended beyond the immediate situation. "It was a personnel matter," he told Jim. "It happens. You can't always judge a person until they get on the job. What you need to do is get the right controls in place so something like this doesn't happen again."

In the aftermath of the embezzlement, Jim's time and attention shifted further away from the program areas where he excelled. Entire yellow tablets were now dedicated to follow-up tasks like organizing a forensic audit of financial records, submitting claims to insurance and credit card companies, and discussing potential criminal charges with local prosecutors. The highest priority was assigned to tedious follow-up work in each of these areas, such as making information available and answering questions. In the end, Hugworks was able to recoup $70,000 through insurance policy and credit card company coverage, but the damage had been done—and the difficulties Hugworks faced were a problem for KidLinks as well. The KidLinks board was beginning to realize that Hugworks may need to be managed very differently to ensure confidence in how the money KidLinks sent Hugworks was being handled.

*****

The program side of Hugworks had grown during the prior ten years. While live therapeutic music sessions at local hospitals and care centers remained their primary activity, Jim and Paul were always on the lookout for more songs to add to the growing library. Music therapy sessions conducted by board-certified practitioners were added in 2006 to extend direct services beyond the hospitals and lend credibility to Hugworks' hallmark TME discipline. "We thought, *We know these music therapists and they do great work. We know the value of music therapy for kids. It is an established discipline. Adding this will show people we are serious*," said Jim.

Following the suggestion from a board member who was a professor of early childhood education, work had begun on a leaders' guide to help teachers and daycare center workers use Hugworks songs as a teaching tool. Animated versions of the most popular songs in the repertoire engaged these audiences more deeply with the music. Jim and Paul saw these additional programs as spokes on the Hugworks brand wheel—ways to reach more people with their songs and services. Ideas were coming in from all angles, and staff and board members found it easy to say yes to them all.

Through it all, the KidLinks Foundation continued significant support for Hugworks, with annual events and ad hoc support of specific projects. At the same time, less funding was coming in from individual donors due to increased competition from charities supported by more sophisticated marketing efforts. "There was just never enough money," said Jim.

Many nonprofit organizations fail to have adequate resources to achieve their missions, making it critical to avoid developing programs that extend beyond its core pursuit. It is difficult to say that mission creep had become an issue for Hugworks, but the symptoms were there. New initiatives had led to the need for greater funding. More projects were competing for limited available dollars. Additional organizational complexity demanded increased management time and attention. Resources and staff were stretched thin, leading to projects bogging down or never reaching completion. Hugworks had fallen into what might be called the "nonprofit catch-22," where so much time and effort are dedicated to fundraising to achieve its mission that the organization's attention is distracted from accomplishing that mission.

*****

Adam Hall joined the KidLinks Foundation board in 2011. As a principal and executive vice president of an insurance and risk management firm that serviced oil and gas operators, the board assignment satisfied his desire for networking opportunities with others in his industry. But KidLinks basically just held two events each year, paid the expenses, and then gave what was left to Hugworks and local hospitals. After a couple years, Adam realized he wanted to become involved more directly in nonprofit work. After J.W. suggested Hugworks as a possible fit, Adam met with Jim and took the time to see what he was doing for the children in the hospital. When the invitation came to join the Hugworks board, Adam jumped at the chance. "I joined because I was really drawn to their mission," he said.

Adam's dual assignment made him a perfect liaison between the two organizations. It also gave him the opportunity to see firsthand the inner workings of the Hugworks board. "I realized that I was stepping into something that had been around for a number of years, so I spent a lot of time listening and getting to know that board and how the organization operated," Adam explained.

In due time, Adam could see that changes were needed. "KidLinks board meetings were short and to the point," said Adam. "But when I sat in a Hugworks board meeting, I saw very quickly that there was stress, a constant push-and-pull there. They were on a shoestring budget, and there were differences of opinion on what to do on a month-to-month basis, even on the most insignificant issues."

As the KidLinks board started planning for its next event, members voiced concerns about whether the money they were raising was going to the right places. "We didn't see the level of sophistication needed to operate given the dollar amounts KidLinks was giving them," said Adam. As businesspeople, the KidLinks board coalesced around what seemed an obvious next step. They agreed to provide the capital for Hugworks to conduct a comprehensive business plan. "We could see they did not have the business structure to accommodate growth," said J.W. "Every organization needs a road map to point out the areas that need attention if you want to grow." The KidLinks Foundation's role was moving beyond monetary gifts and into offering businesslike direction on how Hugworks should operate.

Over the next year, the KidLinks board continued to discuss a range of options on how to manage the relationship with its primary partner. Discontinue funding Hugworks? Establish conditions that Hugworks would need to meet to continue to receive funding? Or something else? Two firm conclusions emerged from these discussions:

- The Hugworks mission was one the KidLinks Foundation would continue to support.

- The current Hugworks organization lacked the necessary systems and structure, given the dollar amounts KidLinks was providing.

"What we saw didn't deter us in supporting them," said J.W. "We still believed that what they were doing was great. But there was something in that mix that wasn't quite right."

A series of unfortunate events and ongoing debates had created difficulties that were bringing Hugworks to a breaking point. KidLinks had invested too much effort and money in the main beneficiary of its fundraising machine to sit back and watch. Something had to be done to change the current trajectory, but what?

CHAPTER THIRTEEN

A New Narrative

More often than you might imagine, innovation comes through people who know little about the subject because they possess what is called a "beginner's mind." For example, twenty-six-year-old Vernon Hill was not a banker, but his experience scouting real estate locations for new McDonald's restaurants made him wonder why banks were not as accessible and convenient as other retail establishments. Based on that insight, Hill launched Commerce Bank in 1973, which introduced retail basics like consistent brand look and extended hours to an industry known for its stuffy image and lack of flexibility.

Edwin Land may have possessed expertise in developing optic filters for sunglasses, but it was an innocent question from a three-year-old that triggered his most famous innovation. While on vacation, Land took a picture of his daughter, who asked why the camera couldn't produce the picture immediately. Three years later, the Land Camera was introduced, making it possible for a picture to be taken and developed in less than a minute. As a result of this self-developing film innovation, Polaroid sold millions of these cameras between 1948 and 1983.

In Zen Buddhism this concept is known as *shoshin*, which refers to approaching a subject, even one familiar to you, with an attitude of openness. When you are a beginner at something, which happens to children much of the time, you are more open to new information and what might be done with it. In his book *Zen Mind, Beginner's*

Mind, Shunryu Suzuki writes, "In the beginner's mind there are many possibilities, but in the experts there are few."

Grant Hollingsworth was a banking veteran but a "beginner" in the nonprofit world when he became a member of the Hugworks board in 2008. His résumé has the markings of a solid banking career. After receiving a master's degree in economics and business finance from the University of Texas, he worked as a lobbyist for a major national gas transporter before moving to Texas Bank and Trust in Houston, where he was executive vice-president in charge of lending.

That may be how his bio reads, but according to reliable sources Grant was a force to reckon with far beyond what you might expect from your typical banker. In the wake of the savings and loan crisis of the 1980s, Grant's job was to clean up and collect problem loans made by problem banks. His reputation as a "bulldog problem solver" spread throughout Texas and Louisiana. When banks encountered issues like balance sheets that didn't balance or loans that were about to default, Grant would bring all the key parties into the same room and tell them, "We're here to figure out a solution. You can let me do it on my own, or we can do it together." When he sensed someone was shading the truth, Grant would tell them that was B.O.B.: a "bucket of baloney." Grant Hollingsworth was a man of action who possessed persuasive powers and the force of character to get things done.

But when given a chance to speak about his accomplishments, Grant's voice is that of a humble servant: "I'm not a rich guy, just a good ol' country banker." Inquire about his personal success, and he starts bragging about his grandson Noel's accomplishments on and off the basketball court: "He was unusual for an athlete. He was also a genius." Mention the insight he shared that inspired a new direction for Jim's organization, and he talks about their friendship: "I was supporting Jim Newton, not Celebration Shop. We have walked a lot of miles together."

Grant's association with Jim began before the latter's musical mission shifted its focus toward hospitalized children. Grant and his wife were members of a church where Jim served as youth director while attending seminary. Since he was a banker, Grant lent money to Jim when he needed some. "You don't normally make loans to preachers because they're not a good risk," said Grant. "I was prepared to pay off his loans if it came to that, but I never had to. He always kept his word." Over the years, Grant became a major supporter of Hugworks through numerous personal financial contributions.

An avid follower of his grandson's basketball career, Grant wasn't certain how he would keep up with the lad's hardcourt feats after he enrolled at the Massachusetts Institute of Technology (MIT) in the fall of 2008. A solution arrived when students at the top-notch technical school put their heads together to design a program that allowed those who couldn't be there in person to watch the action. Since the school was already filming the games for players to view later, all that was needed was a way to provide family and friends live access on their home computers. "It's hard to imagine given what we can do today, but streaming wasn't even known back then," said Grant. "I just had to log on to the MIT website and I could watch the game. My wife and I would watch every game."

By his own admission, as a banker he was pretty naïve about how nonprofit programs were developed and run. At one meeting after he had been on the board for a couple years, there was a discussion about ways to increase the number of contacts Jim and Paul had with children in the hospitals. "I didn't know anything about that. But I listened," said Grant. The next day, Grant made a connection that would illuminate the innovation path forward for the Hugworks program delivery model. "I thought, *If I can watch my grandson's basketball games on a computer from fifteen hundred miles away, maybe we can do something like that so kids in the hospitals can listen to our songs.*"

The idea took root after Grant shared it with Jim and the rest of the Hugworks board. An online platform could provide virtual access to the Hugworks songs whenever and wherever severely ill children and their caregivers wanted it. By providing hospitals with digital access to their music, Hugworks could reach countless more children and caregivers than were being served via Jim's and Paul's in-person visits, making it a perfect fit with their mission "to bring the healing power of music to kids everywhere." The idea leveraged the team's core competency in creating songs containing messages kids needed to hear. Users could create customized playlists that fit their interests and age. The program used technology to reach children through digital media devices that were becoming their preferred way to access music, demonstrating the organization's ability to keep up with the changing times.

In addition to the impressive list of benefits, online access to Hugworks music partially addressed a concern that the KidLinks Foundation board had discussed for quite some time. A few years earlier, one of its more influential members asked, "If Jim and Paul have an accident on the road, what happens to Hugworks? What is the succession plan?" J.W. spoke to Jim regarding the matter but left uncomfortable that no clear plan was in place. "Let's try to figure out a more definitive, clear path, because I need to talk to the KidLinks trustees not only about what you are doing now but also how you are planning for the future," he told Jim.

But it wasn't just the future of Jim or Paul or Hugworks that worried J.W. He was harboring the same concern regarding the KidLinks Foundation he helped found. He had tried to get some of the younger businesspeople involved in leadership but it was always an uphill challenge. When he complained to a friend that the younger people weren't stepping up, the friend told J.W., "They are just like you were at that age—chasing a career and raising a family. Maybe they'll be ready to help lead when they get older, but not now."

Beyond the shared succession planning issue, the KidLinks board was beginning to realize the degree to which the two organizations had become codependent. Hugworks could not survive without the financial support of KidLinks, and KidLinks had no clear purpose without a successful Hugworks. A series of negative incidents, like the embezzlement, exposed the need for Hugworks to adopt rigorous business practices. Without total confidence in how the funds were being handled, the KidLinks Foundation concluded it was not being a good steward of the resources generated. After discussing a wide range of options, the board came to the conclusion that the only way to make the relationship work was to merge the two organizations and run it using responsible, for-profit business practices and approaches. The upside opportunity was too great to not pursue; the risks of doing nothing were too high to ignore.

Respecting Jim's feelings would be critical to the process, so J.W. approached him first. His message was as simple as it was compelling. "What do you think about merging our two organizations? We have good business heads and a couple fundraising events going. We don't run any programs, but that's what you guys do well. Maybe we would be stronger if we came together." Jim responded he would bless it from a founder's perspective. "I was gung-ho about it." Others key to the process also expressed strong support, like Janice Kane, who was Hugworks board chair at the time. She told J.W. a merger was the best idea she had heard in a long time. "It made a lot of sense since our main supporter was the KidLinks Foundation and they existed only to support us, so why not merge the two and become a lot stronger?"

*****

A merger of equals takes place when two entities combine to form a new structure that integrates them. This legal term also captures the spirit behind bringing Hugworks and KidLinks under the same organizational umbrella. There was no disputing that a merger would take advantage of their complementary competencies. The high level of trust that already existed between key players made the idea feel like a natural extension of their historic partnership.

The process moved quickly with J.W. in the driver's seat. He sent a proposal letter to Janice dated October 23, 2014, that laid out key conditions to be satisfied for the merger to take place. Among the major items were as follows:

- J. W. Brown, Janice Kane, and Adam Hall would continue to serve as board members of the new organizations.

- All other board members of the existing organizations would resign their positions and a new seven-member board be selected.

- Terms of employment would continue for Jim Newton and Paul G. Hill.

- An executive director would be selected within the initial twelve months of operation.

- An independent accounting firm identified by the KidLinks Foundation would be engaged.

- The new organization would use their best efforts to sell the current Hugworks office building.

The deadline to complete the transaction was set for December 31, 2014, a little more than two months away. "I thought it was really fast, but J.W. made it happen," said Janice. The merger of Hugworks and the KidLinks Foundation became official on January 2, 2015. The new entity retained the KidLinks name to provide continuity with supporters who attended their fundraising events in the past.

*****

The year 2015 was one of transition for the new organization. While J.W., Adam, and Janice remained on the board, new members from legal and business backgrounds were recruited to tackle difficult governance issues. Diana Crawford was hired as chief executive officer early in the year, bringing proven leadership abilities to the team.

The digital platform named Hugworks Children's Network was launched that fall, providing free access to the large catalog of helpful and healing songs. During the next two years, eighty-five new songs were added to the site, many from outside artists willing to share their content.

A new channel was added in 2016 that offers resources for music therapists and families.

An improved, more user-friendly version of the platform launched in 2018 with capabilities to support continued expansion of content and applications. At the same time, the original Hugworks Children's Network name was dropped to avoid confusion with the KidLinks organization name. New songs, animations, and instructional videos continue to be added to the growing catalog of resources at www. KidLinks.org.

Today, the combined organization looks and operates much differently than the one-man show Jim started over forty years ago. A board of directors comprising individuals from business backgrounds sets priorities and ensures that activities are aligned with overall goals and fit within budgetary constraints. A comprehensive marketing strategy built upon the unique elements of the KidLinks brand adds clarity on key target audiences going forward. A new generation of officers has assumed key leadership responsibilities, allowing J.W. to play critical advisory and mentor roles. Jim has transitioned into the role of "founder," with many of his former responsibilities handled by new professional staff. Jim and Paul continue to pursue new songs containing positive content, share their music through in-person visits, and conduct virtual and live events. In sum, KidLinks is managed today using the sound business practices donors expect and the mission deserves.

KidLinks remains devoted to providing healing, hope, and happiness through music and media for children everywhere. Consistent with that mission, recent efforts have focused on expanding the number of partner organizations as a way for more children to access their unique and helpful content. For example, in 2020 KidLinks launched the Social-Emotional Skills resource—a customized music platform that supports clinicians and families in the development of coping and social skills in children. The stage is now set for KidLinks to continue to find ways to provide stateof-the-art services for children who need unconditional love and acceptance—which the power of therapeutic music can bring.

Adam Hall and Janice Kane, who both remained on the board of the new KidLinks organization during its first two years, are perhaps best positioned to assess the outcome of the merger. Looking back seven years later, their words are almost interchangeable as they describe three important reasons why the merger was the right thing to do.

- It was a matter of survival.

I think it was successful in the sense that I don't know how long Hugworks could have survived in its current form. I think it may have run out of steam. —Adam

Hugworks wouldn't be here now if we hadn't done the merger. —Janice

- It opened the organization up to new possibilities.

A lot of the long-term partners had been asking us, "What is new? What is next?" The merger gave us a new narrative. We could go back and say, "Here's what we're doing." It gave donors a shot in the arm at a time when we were scrambling to find new supporters and develop new relationships. —Adam

It enabled us to grow and find different ways to provide services which probably would not have come to fruition without the merger. —Janice

- It honored Jim's legacy.

It was about carrying on a legacy, so we needed to do it the right way. —Adam

We saw it as Jim's legacy. We saw this as the way to make that happen. —Janice

*****

In 2013, Grant Hollingsworth shared an insight that set into motion an organizational transformation far beyond what he could have ever imagined at the time. Jim Newton in 2020 described Grant's impact this way:

> **I give thanks that we had a generous board member and donor, Grant Hollingsworth, who had the vision to suggest that we develop an online platform for kids and families. It is very gratifying to know that many, many children, families—and even healthcare and education professionals—have unlimited access to KidLinks' therapeutic music entertainment and music therapy resources which foster healing, hope and happiness every day, around the clock. Thank you, Grant, for giving us the inspiration and guidance to become who we are today. (from the KidLinks Mission Moment, 2020)**

True to form, Grant describes his contribution with humility and in a folksy manner that reflects his genuine and humble spirit. "I didn't really do much. I just made a connection between watching my grandson's games and the need to build up the number of contacts Jim and Paul had with children in the hospitals. You know, even a blind pig finds an acorn every now and then."

THE IMPACT

CHAPTER FOURTEEN

The Stories She Could Tell

The first time Jim cradled her in his arms he knew they were a perfect match. Part of the attraction was her shape—broad shoulders and curves in all the right places, accentuated by her long and slender neck adorned with mother of pearl. But it was her deep, resonant tone, providing the perfect complement to Jim's baritone voice, that defined her appeal. "Brunhilda is a miracle," Jim said. They are still together almost forty-five years after they first met.

Brunhilda has had other admirers through the years. On one occasion, Jim and Paul were playing for a group of children in a hospital playroom when a reluctant toddler left the security of his mother's lap to dance with the music. As they ended their last song, the child came forward and planted a huge kiss on Jim's guitar and walked away without saying a word. According to Jim, "Brunhilda never received such a blessing!"

Technically, Brunhilda is a Guild model F-412 BLD, which is code for its jumbo body with top, back, and sides all constructed out of blond maple wood. Jim was attracted to the twelve-string model because of the sonic qualities the six pairs of strings produced, the lower four tuned in octaves while the upper two are in unison. "With the twelve-string, I can play easy chords but sound like a better guitar player than I am because all of those harmonics are in there. I always loved that tone." As for her name, "There was no thought process behind it," said Jim. "I thought it would be cute and silly. I have no idea how I came up with it."

Guitars usually spend most of their time quietly tucked away in their cases waiting for their owner to pick them up. But Brunhilda has been Jim's loyal sidekick since he bought her for $700 in 1977 (more than $3,000 in current dollars). Brunhilda was there when Jim sang for Toby and his mother in 1983 and has been with him every day since. "It is still a great guitar," said Jim. "She looks her age because of all the cracks and nicks all over it, but she still sounds wonderful."

When Jim started bringing Brunhilda and his songs to hospitals in the early 1980s, research that demonstrated the benefits of music in clinical settings—such as lowered blood pressure, reduced heart rate, pain management, distraction, memory stimulation, and so on—would be years in the future. Like pioneers in most disciplines, Jim received challenges from those who doubted his service through song was anything special. "It's just music, right?" skeptics might ask.

Jim had a consistent response to those who doubted music's efficacy as a healing modality. "Take some time out of your day and come see for yourself," he said. "That is how you can tell that what we do makes a difference." Jim must have been right. J. W. Brown, Adam Hall, Janice Kane, that anonymous businessman, and numerous others who accepted Jim's invitation to join him during hospital visits became his most ardent supporters.

There have been times when Jim wished Brunhilda could express herself in ways that stretched beyond chords and arpeggios, that she could speak to what she had seen over the years. But since that was not possible, Jim, Paul, and others have done the writing for her. The following vignettes, written from the perspective of those providing their service of music, offer firsthand accounts of the immense range of beneficial responses music elicits when offered to those in pain and suffering. Or, as Jim would say, "They show that it works!"

REAL MEN DO CRY

The sixteen-year-old boy rolling his IV pole down the hall perked up when we asked if we could sing him a song. We moved to a small sitting area at the end of the hall and sang "One Day at a Time." When we finished, the young man said, "That song really fits my life. It says just how I feel!" He began to quietly cry and continued, "It's so hard. I've been fighting this cancer now for fifteen years!" Then he cried some more. We told him it must really be tough to go through his illness. He apologized for "breaking down" and we assured him that real men *do* cry and that he was honoring us by sharing his feelings and his tears. What a privilege it is to be invited into the young lives of the courageous kids we meet, and to be able to employ the spiritual and emotional power of music to make a difference in their lives!

A VISIT TO THE ER

We were finishing up our day with a visit to the emergency room of a children's hospital. When we walked in, we could tell it had been a tough shift by the looks on the staff's faces. The head nurse told us, "We really need your music more than ever today. A child died in the ER this morning."

We moved from room to room and sang songs for eight children and their parents. When we were done singing for all the children, we went to the nurses' station and sang for ten to twelve nurses and doctors who displayed smiles and tears as they swayed to the music and clapped their hands. When we left thirty minutes or so after we arrived, they thanked us again and again for coming to their unit that day.

A SONG FOR A BALLERINA

I (Paul) knocked quietly on the room of a ten-year-old girl, poked my head inside, and asked if the patient would like a song. Her mom informed me that she was asleep. I began excusing myself and backing out of the room when the mom said, "But I'd like a song. I know she will hear it. Music is magic in that way." *Wow*, I thought. *Someone who understands the power of music.*

I decided to play a soft song titled "Ballerina" that I had written for my own daughter many years ago. After the first verse the mom's eyes started to moisten, and by the time the last lines finished, she was weeping silently. It was as if a wave of understanding had allowed her to open up the channel of her feelings and allow the tears to flow. She told me her daughter also liked ballet and had ballet shoes. Who knew?

ALONE AND CRYING

We approached the room and found a six-month-old in her crib all alone. She was lying on her side and crying softly. There was recorded music playing in the background, but we decided to add a little live sound to the room. We played our song softly, but it seemed to cut through the other distractions. Before we finished, she had rolled over, searching the room for the point from which this new element had entered her world. Her crying had stopped, and the monitors showed that her heart rate had eased.

CAUSING A SCENE

As we were making the rounds today, we entered a floor where four women were gathered at the nurses' station. One of them lit up when she saw our guitars and said, "Oh boy, music. Are you going to play us a song?" We weren't sure if she was kidding, but we took the opportunity to bring a little levity to their afternoon. We began playing "Stand by Me," and they began clapping their hands and singing along. One particularly enthusiastic maintenance worker began dancing and kicking her legs up in the air. It was a joyous moment. People who passed through the hall at that time also found a reason to smile at the scene.

LITTLE DRUMMER BOY

At one of our room visits today there was a young boy who already had a smile on his face when we entered. We handed him a shaker, and the smile grew even bigger as he began to shake it in anticipation of what was coming. And then when the music began, everything within his reach became an instrument. He turned his empty cup upside down for a drum and used both his fingers to tap on it. He then banged the cup itself up and down on his tray. It was as if he couldn't find enough objects to include in his percussion ensemble. We left knowing our brief time had given him the opportunity to immerse himself completely in his own self-expression.

RESPECT

We were doing bedside visits, and as we went into the room of a little five-year-old boy we noticed a few doors down a doctor making rounds with six or seven interns, residents, and nurses. We had just introduced ourselves to the young boy and were about to begin playing when the entire medical group moved to our doorway. We asked the head doctor if they needed us to let them see the boy first. She said, "No, we came to hear you. What you provide is more healing than anything we will do with him today!" So we played and sang, and the little boy, along with the gaggle of medical pros, clapped and danced along. Everyone respects the healing power of music!

SPECIAL FRIENDS

We were singing and playing relaxing songs in the oncology infusion waiting area when some women came in with three pet therapy dogs. We continued to play quietly. When the women were done visiting with the kids, we asked if we could sing a special song for their canine friends. We sang "Lemme Be Your Friend," a song we recorded written from the perspective of a dog singing to its owner. These wonderful folks were tearing up as they thought about how their very own beloved pets might be singing that message to them. When we were done, we thanked each other for bringing our various talents to the hospital to benefit the kids and families.

KICKING TO THE BEAT

Today we visited the room of a fourteen-month-old girl. She was lying awake but listless in her crib. After we started to play and sing, she began to kick her legs to the beat of our song. A cute smile came across her little face. Her mom got up from where she was sitting just beaming and began to take pictures of her little one. The commotion drew several nurses to the door, and they began to dance along to the music. Is there any wonder why we love what we do?

UNBLOCKING BARRIERS

A couple of weeks ago, we were doing our monthly sing-along at a special-care residential shelter that serves moms and kids. We began to play and sing a song of comfort and relaxation called "Circle of Friends," and almost immediately one mom put her head in her hands and began to shed silent tears. Her kids were enjoying the rhythm shakers and the song and didn't seem to notice.

Music connects with our heart and spirit and can release pent-up feelings, helping them pour forth from deep inside. This healthy expression of feelings will many times unblock the barriers we have to comfort, peace, and even happiness. By the end of our session, this mom was smiling and singing along with her kids. What an honor it is to bring this musical magic to folks who need it the most.

GIVING AND RECEIVING

I (Paul) was visiting a hospital on my own when I was taken into the intensive care unit to sing to a child less than two years old. I have learned that in situations like this, a relaxing and quiet song works best. As I played "If I Could," the child stared intently with a look that I could only interpret as curiosity. When I reached the last verse and sang, "If I could, I would give a smile to you," as if by magic the child broke into a wide smile, which brought a smile to me as well. In that moment, I realized the song had been fulfilled when I sang the closing line, "I know you've given more than one to me."

FUTURE GUITAR STAR

I think I met a future guitar player at the hospital today. A fifteenmonth-old boy was slowly moving down the hall with his mother and a nurse. I got down on my knees so I could sing for him at something close to his eye level. Early in the song he became so engaged in the music that he reached out and started strumming the strings on my guitar. One never knows maybe he'll become famous someday. Or maybe he will bring his own caring music to some hospital when he grows up. I hope it's the latter.

STILL SINGING

At our last room visit today, we sang one of our favorite songs, titled "Inside," to a five-year-old girl and her mother. The child listened intently to the lyrics of each verse and chorus, which repeats the line "Inside, inside, that's the most important part." After we said goodbye and were only a few steps away from their room, the mother poked her head out their door and called out, "She's still singing, 'Inside, inside!'"

CONNECTING

Sometimes what we see can be hard to handle, like when we entered a young boy's room where his mother, grandmother, and a nurse were gathered closely around his bed. The boy was having intermittent seizures every fifteen seconds or so and throwing up into a little pan they held for him. As we began to sing a very relaxing song, he focused his eyes directly on us. After each time he would seize, he would then reconnect with us. After the first two choruses, he was mouthing the words with us, a sign he was really connecting with the music and the message. As we completed the song, the boy said in a quiet, hoarse voice, "Thank you."

HE NEVER SAW IT COMING

As I (Jim) walked down the hall during room visits today, I heard a little boy crying loudly. I stuck my head into a room where a four-year-old was with his parents and a nurse who was holding him down for a needle stick. I said, "Want me to try some relaxing music?" They all looked at me and eagerly nodded yes. I began to softly play and sing, and the little one turned his head to see what the sound was and immediately began to calm down. Distracted by the song, he never saw the shot coming or felt its pain.

A SPECIAL KIND OF LAUGH

We sang for a little baby in a long-term rehab unit today while her grandfather was playing with her on the floor. As we began a soft, relaxing song, at first the little girl just looked at us. But then she began to giggle and laugh out loud. It was that kind of laugh that parents and grandparents (and even strolling musicians) love to hear in their kids.

BIG CHEEKS

We were fortunate to have the opportunity to sing with a mom and her four-year-old boy today. He had been nauseated from chemo treatments and he was beginning to feel better when we arrived. His cute little face was still very swollen from the medication but he had his Mickey Mouse guitar slung around his neck and played along with us. It looked like his smile would burst through those little cheeks! His mother beamed too, but with tears in her eyes.

CHILDREN OF ALL AGES

After singing with a critically ill adolescent today, we had a visit with his grandmother in a different room down the hall. She shared her concern about her grandson, and also about a good friend of more than forty years who was being treated in an adult ward in the same hospital. She asked us to sing a relaxing song, and we selected "Weave," which is about how our lives and our memories become woven together. After the first verse, she began to cry quietly. We visited more after the song, and she thanked us for helping to lift her spirits during a very difficult time. It was wonderful to see how our outreach helps "children" of all ages!

NOURISHING TUNES

We sang for a preemie in her room as a hospital volunteer was feeding her a bottle. When we completed our soft, relaxing song, the volunteer told us she'd been having trouble getting the baby to take her bottle. She said, "You can't believe how much the song relaxed her and she immediately began to nurse."

SYNCHRONICITY

When we approached the open door to the room, it appeared the nurse was preparing for some procedure, which is usually an indication it is not a good time for us to offer a song. But the nurse said, "This is a great time! You can play music while we give him his chemo."

We entered the room to find a young patient about twelve years old, along with his parents. We asked them if it was okay for us to play some music during the procedure, and they assured us it was. The mother explained that her son had been trying to determine what to do for his science fair project and had decided to observe the effect that music might have on someone undergoing chemotherapy treatment. Today was his first round of an anticipated yearlong process. We were shocked. We come to this hospital only one day each year and we happened to arrive at very moment he was beginning his treatment? His tearful mother expressing her thanks to us in the hall afterward shared her own theory: synchronicity of the universe was in play at that moment.

*****

Around the time Jim and Brunhilda had been visiting hospitals together for over twenty-five years, Jim's lifelong friend David Hahn wrote a poem honoring the twelve-string companion. While he never used her given name in the piece, David captured in first person Brunhilda's unique vantage point in the poem's closing lines:

I have loved the journey,

I have seen more tears and suffering than most will witness in a hundred lifetimes,

And yet it has been full of more meaning, inspiration, and joy than most will ever know.

CHAPTER FIFTEEN

Voices from the Other Side of the Guitar

Because there was no easy or appropriate way to solicit formal feedback from the people served during their visits, Jim and Paul were intentional about capturing what they witnessed. The stories they offered (from Brunhilda's perspective) demonstrate the immediate and positive impact that live therapeutic music can have on children and families dealing with the challenges associated with severe illness. While the observations of those offering the service is informative, what those on the other side of the guitar saw and felt provides undeniable evidence regarding the power of music to help and heal.

The following stories represent a sample of the hundreds of letters and emails written from the perspective of those who heard and saw Paul and Jim over the years. Because these messages and letters from individuals who received or witnessed Jim and Paul's gift of music were unsolicited, they represent testimony of the most powerful and credible kind. In most cases, these messages arrived months and years later, demonstrating the enduring impact that therapeutic music had on kids and families.

FROM A PEDIATRIC PATIENT EIGHTEEN YEARS LATER

I first saw Jim and Paul perform in the summer of 1993 as a newly diagnosed childhood cancer patient at a camp for children like myself. I recall how their music encouraged me to sing along with others, helping release me from my shy shell and get to know my fellow campers. These moments of shared song helped to foster friendships that are still valued today, nearly two decades after camp.

Now I work as a child life specialist, providing therapeutic play and counseling for children with HIV. Recently I was given the opportunity to host Jim and Paul in my clinic, where they shared their music with my patients. I was honored that they remembered me and how far I've come since my illness. More importantly, I was thrilled to learn that the songs and their loving voices were the same. For my patients, it was a fun respite and a moment when they could dance. For me, it was a testament to how seemingly small gifts such as a song could be a timeless companion.

It is my honor to continue sharing their music with my patients and families in an effort to provide them with the same joyful companionship.

FROM A GRATEFUL MOM

I just want to thank you for what I know was a happy and healing experience for our son, hearing your music and seeing you play. You lifted his spirits. I want him to have the chance to hear you all singing some more, so I am glad we can have the CDs to listen to also. You see many patients, I am sure, and I wanted to just reach out personally and tell you that even a short visit means a ton to all of us.

Even though this journey has been so hard and has had many scary moments, we feel truly blessed by all the wonderful and kind people we have met and by all the kindness we have witnessed. We are very hopeful for our son's total healing and return to normal toddler life! All our best, and with gratitude.

FROM AN OLDER SISTER YEARS LATER

Growing up I never really had a way to express myself. I felt like I was pushed aside because I was the sibling of a child with cancer. I held so much anger and pain inside, never understanding why my little brother and best friend had to be sick all the time. I felt that because he was sick, I was being ignored.

After attending cancer patient camp with my brother back in the early nineties, I found my release. Because of Jim and Paul and their music, I found a way to express my feelings through song lyrics. Their song "If I Could" somehow found a way to my soul and has never left it. Jim and Paul were the ones who inspired me and gave me hope, and a new way to express myself through words. They might not realize it, but through their music they have inspired a lot of children and given them so much hope and faith.

In 1993, I lost my little brother to osteosarcoma. Because of all the emotions that were bottled up inside of me, I started to write a song for him. After almost ten years, I finished it—and who would have known that the same year I would be returning to camp as a counselor and that I would be able to share my song with Jim and Paul. I honestly believe they are angels sent here to help children with no hope left to find hope and believe that there is something wonderful out there. Jim and Paul are wonderful, and I hope that they continue to share their beautiful words with children all over the world who need to hear what they are singing about. You guys are my inspiration, and I thank you for that!

FROM A PEDIATRIC PATIENT TEN YEARS LATER

I think about your songs all the time. I can't remember the name, but my favorite song said, "If you can't run, you can walk, if you can't walk, you can crawl." I went to sleep Christmas 2000 and woke up two months later a paraplegic. I regained total mobility and I live a normal life now. Your songs helped heal my spirit. There is no doubt about it. You are a blessing to every torn spirit that hears your music.

FROM A CHILD LIFE SPECIALIST

Your empathy, patience, creativity, imagination, and attitude speak volumes to everyone whose lives you touch. I hope you realize the difference you make. One of our patients is a five-year-old little boy who has recently undergone surgery for a significant brain tumor. He has been in the hospital for months and has had a difficult road of healing. The day that you came to perform was the first time that he had visited the playroom since his surgery. He was quite overwhelmed at first. After a while, he was holding his shaker and making music, too. His parents and our staff were ecstatic to see the progress he had made. Without your being there, this breakthrough may have taken much longer. Thank you for easing his healing process.

The tears, the smiles, the laughter we share confirm the importance of music in our lives. The music you share allows kids and their families to enter the human emotional experience in a nonthreatening manner and freely express what they are feeling. On behalf of our children, their families and the staff, thank you for sharing your gifts. We love you!

FROM A PARENT THIRTEEN YEARS LATER

Your visits to the hospital and the CDs meant the world to our son, who was fighting a battle with cancer which he eventually lost. He loved listening to music. He would listen to music all day, and we constantly listened to music in the car on our many trips to the doctor, the hospital, or to therapies. I cannot tell you how much joy you and your music brought to our son during his short life. We still, tearfully though happily, remember some of your songs. Thanks for brightening all our days and for providing so much to all the special children.

FROM THE MOTHER OF A LITTLE BOY

I know I will not be able to fully express our thanks for letting us use your "Peaceable Kingdom" for our son's memorial service. But when I heard it at the hospital, I knew that it was something I liked. I had hoped and prayed that we wouldn't have to ask you if we could use it. We also would like to have your permission to use a few of the words to put on our son's gravestone. It would help express some of our feelings about our precious son. Thank you ever so much.

FROM A FRIEND AND DONOR

I have been with Jim on a number of hospital visits, starting in the mid-eighties to a pediatric burn unit. I had never been around more than one sick person at a time and I was shocked and demoralized seeing dozens of kids wrapped in skintight bandages. All of the kids in the ward that could walk followed Jim and his beloved twelve-string guitar around the halls like he was a Pied Piper, marching along stiff-legged, looking like little Egyptian mummies! That was about two decades ago—but I can still close my eyes and see every detail! The sight of dozens of innocent kids facing a life of unbelievable pain and scarring, just trying to get through one more day, is a sobering reminder of life's unfair fortunes. That day, more than any other in my life, still haunts me. Jim sang and softly told the kids stories and jokes as if we were at recess at the local elementary school. Their muted voices came alive, and their hollow eyes seem to sparkle as Jim sang. His last words to them were, "Hang on—there will be better days ahead."

I mark that spring day, and any other that I get to travel with Jim and Paul, as the best because I know that "better days" for thousands of kids started a long time ago thanks to them.

TO JIM FROM A YOUNG PATIENT

I was hospitalized for four months, and you helped make my time there livable. Even when I couldn't come out of my room, you came in my room and sang to me. I loved that. You made my world not soooo gloomy. My mother enjoyed it too. I guess I just wanted to say thank you for everything you've done for children in hospitals. I think I speak for everyone when I say I love YOU like a big brother!!!!

FROM A HEALTHCARE PROFESSIONAL

The father of one of our chronic patients was weeping. He came up to me to let me know that he was not crying out of sadness, but out of comfort from your music. Your visit was extremely therapeutic for all of us here.

FROM THE MOTHER OF AN INFANT

I wanted to thank you for your visit to the PICU where you sang to my son extra loud since he was sedated and on an extremely noisy respirator. Sadly, he died a few weeks later, but I am glad that he left with a song in his heart. I have listened over and over to "Life Is Aloha," and it brings me much comfort. We even played it at his memorial ceremony. I want to tell you how much we do appreciate the work you do and the music you spread throughout the hospital corridors.

FROM A MOTHER

Thank you for your music. At first, we played your tape on the way home after each chemotherapy session. Now I hear my son singing snatches of songs while he plays, especially, "Doctor, doctor, I know you want to help but sometimes it hurts." Your music has helped him to cope with the changes in his life that leukemia has brought. Thank you for sharing your gift with children.

FROM AN AGENCY PARTNER

It's equally important that we engage our kids' parents. I hear all the time from families how singing KidLinks songs and watching videos is something parents and children are doing together. It's adding one more tool in the parents' toolbox to help them and their kids navigate whatever bump in the road they may be experiencing.

A LETTER TO NOEL "PAUL" STOOKEY

I really like your music. It keeps me going when the treatments aren't going so good. To sing folk music all three of you must be caring people, or at least that is how I feel when I listen to your tapes.

I also like the *Friends of the Family* you did with Jim Newton. Jim came to the cancer camp where I was a camper this past summer. I love the songs "Inside" and "Why Me?" But at seventeen, I try not to ask "why me" because I really won't want anyone else to get cancer.

Noel's note to Jim attached to this letter: "Forward to Jim Newton with love and pride at being associated with you."

FROM A MOTHER

A really beautiful thing happened this morning. This wonderful man was at the hospital today entertaining kids with his music. Such a special way to minister to kids and families! He came to see our daughter, who was in terrible pain and having an awful day. I asked if she'd like him to play a song for her and she gave me a tiny nod. He strummed his guitar and began to gently sing one of my favorite childhood songs by John Denver. I couldn't keep from crying, then I turned to see tears streaming down my mom's face too. I will always remember this moment, and from now on, "For Baby" will be special for us all.

TO JIM FROM A CHILD YEARS LATER

When I was five or six years old, my appendix ruptured while my parents were out of town. By the time they came home, I was very ill. I don't remember much about the hospital stay but I have *vivid* memories of a man coming in and singing to me. We bought one of his cassette tapes and over the years I lost that tape. I contacted the hospital to see if they had records of who performed for me, and they gave me the link to your website. Within moments of playing your video, I was overcome with emotions. It was more powerful than I could have ever expected. I thought I was just finding music that touched me as a child but listening to it for the first time in years made me realize that your music was a part of me. Thank you for helping me and my family through one of the hardest times of our lives.

FROM A PARENT YEARS LATER

How can I make you understand what it means to learn songs about being unique but still normal? Our daughter was walking in the hall in seventh grade when she collapsed, and that was the last time she ever walked. This was our girl who had danced all over our city. We were up at the hospital that time for four months, and I'm sure you can understand why we were pretty depressed. Life had stopped for our family—we did not see how we could go on.

Well, of course, in walks Jim. It is really hard to stay in the blues when someone walks in dragging that guitar, grinning, and saying, "Come on, come on, you're going to come and sing." And I'll never forget that day he sang, "You be you and I'll be me and we'll be together differently." I looked over at my daughter, and she didn't miss a beat of that song. She was laughing and singing, and I realized at that moment we were going to make it! My daughter is different, and life is going to be different, but it is going to be fine. Jim's music found a way in when nobody else could. He gave us hope. He reminded me of the good times just with the songs. He is a lifeline to people like us, parents and children in the medical community.

We lost our daughter this year. Jim came to her celebration of life and sang three of her favorite songs. Until you experience Jim's ministry, you cannot understand the impact it has on us. When you give to this ministry, don't feel sorry for people. Jim's songs teach us that it is OK to be different. They teach us that God still loves us and our world really isn't so bad after all—what a gift! Jim has made us laugh when we had no laughter and taught us that it is okay to cry, too. Know that when you give to KidLinks, your gift endures for a lifetime!

THE FUTURE

CHAPTER SIXTEEN

Music on a Mission

It's tough to make predictions, especially about the future.
—Yogi Berra

Forty years in the service of others. There are countless ways to emphasize that level of ccommitment, such as 16,000 days or 384,000 hours. The most relevant figure might be 450,000, the number of children and caregivers served by KidLinks as of this writing. Knowing that the music was often shared one room and one song at a time, each a single gift of unconditional caring, makes that total even more impressive. The persistence and dedication required to achieve that level of service deserves respect and recognition.

Reaching the forty-year milestone offers everyone involved with KidLinks the opportunity to, at least for a few moments, shift attention from an impressive past to a future full of possibilities. When trying to figure out where you are headed, pausing to remember why you began your journey offers a useful starting point.

Jim Newton's visit with Toby and his mother in March 1983 provided the inspiration for the subsequent four decades of service. Jim considered himself inadequate as he entered their hospital room carrying his guitar. He knew no songs appropriate for the context. Yet somehow, despite all these factors stacked against the situation, his gift of music lifted a gravely ill child out of his pit of suffering, at least for a few moments. In that moment, Jim recognized an unmet human need and realized that music could be a caring modality in ways far beyond what was accepted at the time.

Jim had the natural wisdom to craft a mission statement that would guide him onto his uncharted path of service. Despite a few modest revisions over the next four decades, the mission has always been about bringing the healing power of music to help the children in need. Variations of that statement provided a rational guide for what KidLinks' service would look like, who it served, and how it conducted itself in pursuit of its mission.

As KidLinks looks forward to the next forty years, it is appropriate (perhaps necessary) to consider the higher purpose it hopes to achieve through that mission. This vision statement describes what KidLinks ultimately wants to become and expresses the greater good the organization hopes to serve.

> **Be the most trusted partner in utilizing music as a healing force which transforms the lives of children and their caregivers.**

The following sections delineate how the various elements of this vision statement grow out of KidLinks' history and help guide its path forward.

MOST TRUSTED PARTNER

From the start, Jim understood he could not pursue his passion to help children through his music without the assistance of others. He contacted experts who enriched his understanding of the needs of severely ill children and how he might use music to address them. He established a network of individuals and organizations willing to share their knowledge and skills. These diverse connections tapped into the expertise of the child life community, the sensitivity and songwriting skills of his friend Paul G. Hill, the celebrity status and recording experience of Noel "Paul" Stookey, the business acumen of J. W. Brown, plus countless others. In each case, mutual trust grew into ongoing collaborative relationships that transcended specific projects.

Today, KidLinks has gone a step further by securing formal partnerships with mental health providers that use KidLinks' unique music as a critical component of their clinical services. The KidLinks staff works directly with these agencies to provide customized music and media platforms that allow children and caregivers to develop coping and social skills between formal therapy sessions. Finding innovative ways to collaborate with a wide range of care providers will continue into the foreseeable future. Such ongoing partnerships allow KidLinks to serve as a trusted partner in helping children cope with a wide range of physical, social, and emotional challenges.

UTILIZING MUSIC

It all started with a song, and then a second one before Toby began to respond. When he did, Jim saw how his musical gifts intersected with a deep human need. Over the ensuing forty years, the way KidLinks' recorded music would be delivered evolved from cassette tape to compact disc and now through the KidLinks website. Regardless of how music will be accessed in the future, it must remain central to the KidLinks mission. Building from its past, KidLinks' songs will continue to be preferred over other options because they are intentionally written to contain helpful healing messages and are produced at a level of quality that matches the best commercially-available material.

While the substance of KidLinks' music will remain need-driven, the ways in which it is delivered will continue to evolve. Streaming will inevitably become the most prevalent way to listen to music in the years ahead. Technological advances will allow music to be accessed on demand from anywhere as more devices become able to connect to personalized content that the user selects. In his article "Music in 2030" posted on David Emery Online, music marketing guru David Emery made a highly relevant observation: "If you have access to all the music you could ever wish to 'own,' recommendation and curation [are] vital." This suggests that the rigorous process KidLinks uses to ensure that all songs contain messages that are developmentally appropriate for and therapeutically supportive of all children will become an even more valued characteristic far into the future.

A HEALING FORCE

Jim's intent to make music a healing modality was inspired by instinct, not informed by any known research. He encountered a good deal of skepticism when he suggested four decades ago that music could be a positive, healing force in clinical settings. He could cite no studies to support his ". . . For My Children" initiative, nor any bestselling books to help make the case.

Jim's initial passion was fueled by what he had observed from personal experience regarding the efficacy of the music. He would tell anyone who would listen,

I know it works because I see it in the kid's faces. I know it works because I hear parents talk about it. I know it works because I hear the hospital staff talk about it. I have never wondered whether it was effective or helpful. I don't know how to prove it. If anybody goes with me, they also don't know how to prove it but they know it works, too. It is unmistakable.

Those who made an effort to follow him into hospitals and see therapeutic music in action became the mission's most ardent supporters.

Today, the evidence supporting the healing power of music is as undeniable as it is impressive. A sizeable collection of peer-reviewed research in the music therapy field supports its effectiveness in a wide variety of healthcare and educational settings. While providing a full review would be an imposing task, listed here are just a few of the proven benefits of music interventions, according to the American Music Therapy Association:

- Promoting wellness
- Managing stress
- Alleviating pain
- Expressing feelings
- Enhancing memory

- Improving communication
- Promoting physical rehabilitation

Numerous bestselling books have broadened the understanding of the vast power of music beyond the music therapy community and into the public consciousness. Examples include

- Elena Mannes, *The Power of Music: Pioneering Discoveries in the New Science of Song*
- Daniel J. Levitan, *This Is Your Brain on Music: The Science of a Human Obsession*
- Oliver Sacks, *Musicophilia: Tales of Music and the Brain*
- David Byrne, *How Music Works*
- Frank Fitzpatrick, *Amplified: Unleash Your Potential through the Power of Music*
- Mitchell M. Gaynor, *The Healing Power of Sound*

The evidence and research supporting music as a healing modality are certain to grow larger with time. Music's healing power is embraced as never before—and is being used to change lives by doing so many different things for so many different people. As it looks to the future, KidLinks faces the opportunity to conduct research studies that produce concrete data demonstrating the positive impact of its own therapeutic music entertainment and music therapy programs.

TRANSFORM LIVES

The stories shared in Chapter Fifteen, "Voices from the Other Side of the Guitar," provided a glimpse at music's ability to change lives by offering joy, comforting those who are suffering, providing encouragement, and promoting healing. A noteworthy aspect of these testimonials was how the positive impact remained fresh years later.

One more recent story shared by one of KidLinks' mental health services partners demonstrates music's capacity to help others:

KidLinks is an amazing partner of our children's development program. This partnership allows us to provide the entirety of services needed to ensure that children with special needs can reach their full potential.

When asked to explain the impact of KidLinks' music on the kids we serve, I immediately thought of one little girl. When she started our program as a two-yearold she was nonverbal and nonsocial. She was essentially trapped in her world. She was frustrated that she couldn't express herself. Her demeanor changed when music was played. She would listen attentively and move her body. It wasn't long before she would sing along with Jim and Paul. Music provided a pathway for her to experience her classmates and an avenue to express her feelings.

She is just one of many children who benefit from the power of words, sounds, and music.

KidLinks provides an authentic connection that heals and helps children break through the barriers and form connections.

Going forward, KidLinks will continue to explore applications that advance the ways in which music and media resources are used to make a positive and enduring difference.

CHILDREN AND THEIR CAREGIVERS

While the world of medicine has advanced in ways Jim could never have imagined in 1983, the need for family-centered care is greater today than when he began visiting hospitals. In his original ". . . For My Children" project prospectus from 1983, Jim wrote, "Day by day, kids of all ages are hurting." Despite advances made in modern medicine over the past four decades, the need is as great today as ever.

In early 2020, just prior to the outbreak of the global COVID pandemic, the WHO–UNICEF–Lancet Commission issued a report titled *A Future for the World's Children*, based on the expertise of forty child health specialists from around the world. Authors of this lengthy assessment wrote that today's children face an uncertain future due to socioeconomic, ecological, and political pressures. The authors argued that the needs of children under the age of eighteen should be at the heart of global sustainability efforts. A year and a half later, a press release from UNICEF, "Impact of COVID-19 on Poor Mental Health in Children and Young People 'Tip of the Iceberg,'" warned that the impact of the global pandemic on the mental health and well-being of children would be felt for many years to come:

> **As COVID-19 heads into its third year, the impact on children and young people's mental health and well-being continues to weigh heavily. According to the latest available data from UNICEF, globally, at least 1 in 7 children [have] been directly affected by lockdowns, while more than 1.6 billion children have suffered some loss of education.**

Children's need for access to music and media resources that promote healing by addressing their social and emotional challenges will continue well into the future. Fortunately, there is a growing awareness of music's value as a healing tool. KidLinks is well positioned to meet future demands by offering more avenues for kids and their families to access the healing which its music and media resources provide.

CONCLUSION

KidLinks emerged out of unexpected origins and overcame countless challenges in its relentless passion to provide the healing power of music for children in need. Along the way, KidLinks evolved in unanticipated directions. While no one can know what lies ahead, understanding its rich history, as this book documents, can inform future direction by revealing how KidLinks got to where it is today. By appreciating what Jim, Paul, J.W., Noel, and others have created, future leaders can build a new KidLinks that retains a connection to the past while reinventing itself to remain relevant.

The KidLinks of tomorrow will face opportunities we cannot imagine today that the organization will address in ways we cannot yet fathom. But we can be certain that the two premises upon which KidLinks was founded will remain the reality in the years ahead:

children will continue to be hurting, and music makes a genuine difference. These two truths suggest that KidLinks' pursuit of its vision to "be the most trusted partner in utilizing music as a healing force that transforms the lives of children and their caregivers" will remain as important in the next forty years as it has in the past.

*****

The saga of *Shear Madness*, a play that holds the Guinness World Record for the longest-running nonmusical play in American theater history, offers a cautionary tale that tomorrow's leaders may want to consider. This comedy whodunit is set in the Shear Madness unisex hair salon. During the action, a woman living in the apartment above the salon is murdered and the audience is encouraged to spot the clues and question the suspects, forcing ad-libbed responses from the cast. Late in the play, audience members vote on who they think is guilty. Whoever the audience votes as the murderer then improvises dialogue with the rest of the cast, making the ending of the play different every night.

The final curtain came down on *Shear Madness* in March 2020, two short months after its fortieth anniversary celebration at Boston's Charles Theater—but not because of the onset of the COVID pandemic. The play's unexpected shuttering due to anticipated financial losses provides a sobering reminder that being in business four decades offers no guarantee of continued success.

In the scene inviting the audience to participate in solving the crime, the police detective investigating the case turns to the patrons and says, "Ladies and gentlemen, this is where you come in." In a similar way, new leaders and friends will be given the role of writing the next chapters of the KidLinks story. While an array of paths forward will be open to them, the organization's past offers three storylines for how the future may potentially play out.

STRIVE TO SURVIVE

In this scenario, energy and resources are focused on fundraising efforts to ensure survival. Greater weight is given to following sound business practices than pursuit of the mission. Leaning too far in this direction risks falling prey to what writer Bill E. Landsberg has called— in an article for the *International Journal of Not-for-Profit Law*—the "nonprofit paradox."

> **The business practices the nonprofit embraces to assure its survival threaten to undermine its culture, mission, and public image. In an effort to save its bottom line, the modern nonprofit risks losing its soul.**

PRESERVE THE BALANCE

Here, business principles and pursuit of mission serve complementary roles, mirroring the original intent behind the Hugworks / KidLinks Foundation merger. Leaders find a way to balance passion for the mission with the logic of sound business practices. Heart and head work together as partners. KidLinks board chair Adam Hall described the challenge within this scenario as follows:

> **Sometimes the mission of the organization gets overshadowed by the desire to stay inside the business lines. The problem is, you can start to lose focus on the mission itself and the passion that got us here. . . . I would challenge all of us that, while remaining respectful and professional with each other, we should also have a healthy amount of push and pull between those directly carrying out the mission and those who step in from a board perspective. I think if one gets their way too much it's unhealthy.**

REIGNITE THE PASSION

The healing power of music is the focus and inspiration of this path forward. Value is created by placing in the forefront the needs of those KidLinks serves. The organization places a premium on finding innovative ways for music and media to address the emotional, social, and physical challenges of children and possibly additional audiences. In this scenario, the healing power of music leads the way into uncharted territory.

When asked to reflect on the forty-year journey of service, Jim Newton summed up KidLinks' accomplishments in this way:

> **What we have done, with the help of so many good people, is beyond whatever I could have hoped for. I could never have imagined the details of our success in serving kids, families, and professional caregivers. I just walked through the doors that seemed to open before me.**

New doors will certainly open for the next generation of like-hearted leaders who will need to decide which passageways to walk through and which to avoid.

*****

This chapter started with an epigraph from baseball Hall of Famer and philosopher Yogi Berra. Despite its quaint humor, KidLinks' future leaders will be better served by following President Abraham Lincoln's advice instead: "The best way to predict the future is to create it."

Parroting the detective's challenge to each audience of *Shear Madness*, "Ladies and gentlemen, this is where you come in. Now that you know the story, what will you do to help create the KidLinks of tomorrow, one that continues to take music on a mission?"

CLOSING THOUGHTS

A Circle of Servants

In the year 2022, the nonprofit organization today known as KidLinks began its fortieth year of operation. During the same forty years, thousands of well-intentioned nonprofits opened doors that are now closed. According to the National Center on Charitable Statistics, approximately 30 percent of nonprofits no longer exist after ten years. The likelihood of a nonprofit organization operating as long as KidLinks is exceptionally slim.

KidLinks started as one man's dream with no clear plan and few resources. Yet it continues today using music and media to bring hope and healing to children everywhere. Its longevity raises a question worthy of serious consideration: what can we learn from the KidLinks story that can help other institutions make an enduring mark on those they serve?

I reviewed multiple articles on the subject of nonprofit failures hoping to find an agreed-upon set of issues that KidLinks avoided during its history. But many of the most common reasons cited for failure—lack of business plan, donor lapses, failing to innovate, vacancies in key positions, board-related issues, and so on—had indeed haunted KidLinks at some point during its history. Forces and factors less obvious and more complex must have been in play to explain its longevity.

I recalled reading the bestselling book *Good to Great: Why Some Companies Make the Leap . . . and Others Don't* when it was first released in 2001. The book was the product of Jim Collins and a research team comprising twenty-one students from the Stanford University Graduate School of Business. The goal of their five-year project was to identify the distinguishing characteristics of companies that were able to achieve superior long-term results compared to a set of benchmark companies whose performance lagged.

While their research examined for-profit enterprises, I suspect that many of their conclusions also apply to the nonprofit realm. I found one of their concepts was able to shed light on how an organization with such modest origins as KidLinks could endure for so long. Collins and his team described the "flywheel effect" where superior performance results from the ongoing process of determining what is needed in the current moment and taking the proper action. This concept challenges the assumption that more successful companies achieve their results through a single decision, innovation, or lucky break. This flywheel effect is a form of virtuous cycle—a chain of events where each iteration reinforces the previous one to create momentum that builds with time. That momentum continues in its existing direction until an external factor intervenes and disrupts the pattern. Each step in that process builds upon the prior one, producing balanced and consistent momentum similar to way a flywheel does in engineering applications.

What makes the flywheel effect so illuminating here is how it recognizes the slow, methodical manner in which KidLinks was built—through the cumulative effort of numerous individuals pushing in the same direction. It also demonstrates the power of persistence across time to deliver a positive outcome. As I considered this concept alongside the specifics of the KidLinks story, I saw how it revealed what might be considered the key elements of long-term nonprofit organizational success, what I call here the "Legacy Flywheel."

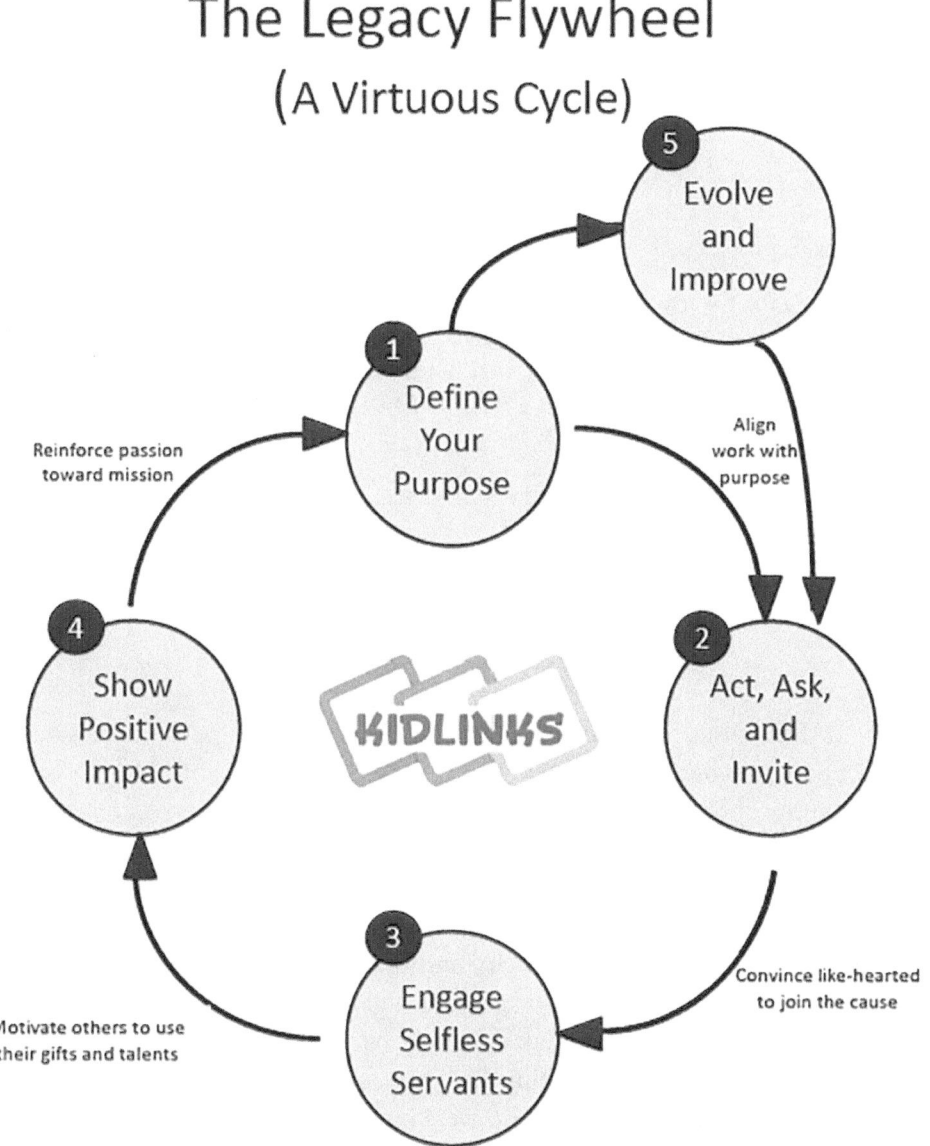

With this framework in mind, let's review what might be considered the CliffsNotes version of the KidLinks story.

DEFINE YOUR PURPOSE

Jim's heart was touched when he sang to Toby and his mother, setting him onto a new path of service. He communicated his intent to hundreds of donors through personal calls and handwritten notes. He articulated his cause with emotional power in the prospectus for what he called his ". . . For My Children" project:

> **Day by day, kids of all ages are hurting, crying, growing more lonely and withdrawn, and little is being done, by any but their families, to comfort them. This is a *real* problem and I am going to do something about it.**

Jim pushed against every challenge, but despite his effort the flywheel of service barely budged. Fueled by his passion and his imagination for what could be, he never gave up.

ACT, ASK, AND INVITE

Although it required a couple years of transition, Jim took decisive action and worked overtime to move into his new mission. He gained the support of his board. He gathered input from a network of experts to understand the depth and breadth of the problem that severely ill children were facing. But Jim also recognized he could not do it alone. He was determined enough to do what he could on his own, smart enough to know he needed help, and brave enough to ask for it. Jim sought out the advice, money, time, and talents of people from all walks of life. He was never afraid to ask because he witnessed the pain the children were experiencing and was confident his music could be their balm. His requests for help were impossible to ignore because his commitment was undeniable in his own actions.

This anecdote from comedian Chris Rock helps to illustrate the point:

> **I used to have horrible cars that would always end up broken down on the highway. When I tried to flag someone down, nobody stopped. But if I pushed my own car, other drivers would get out and push with me. If you want help, help yourself.**

The image of Chris Rock pushing a broken-down car mirrors Jim applying all of his energy to move the cause forward. It was passion in action, making the irrefutable case for others to join him.

ENGAGE SELFLESS SERVANTS

Because he acted and asked, Jim's mission rubbed off on like-hearted people willing to commit their talents and resources. The list is too long to include everyone who leaned in to help the KidLinks Flywheel gain momentum, but a few examples make the point. In each case, what is most revealing is the degree to which they became involved far beyond their original expectations. Noel Stookey assumed he would merely place his stamp of approval on Jim's recording projects, but he became an active writer, singer, and fundraiser. Paul G. Hill was reluctant to apply his skills to children's music until he saw how his compositions helped kids cope with their challenges. J. W. Brown was a consistent but minor donor before he was moved to apply his business experience and acumen to deliver a significant boost to the mission.

That is what a powerful mission is able to do: invite and inspire the right people to share their unique gifts to help shoulder the burden. The occasional bumps and snags encountered along the way may have slowed progress, but they were overcome because selfless servants were willing to help push forward in the same direction and sustain the mission.

SHOW POSITIVE IMPACT

It is one thing to articulate a mission that grabs others at an emotional level. Equally critical is the ability to show others that your work and their support have real impacts. Hitting that sweet spot requires articulating a mission that is compelling *and* achievable.

The transparency and confidence evident in Jim's open invitation for all to "come see for yourself" demonstrated an unequivocal devotion to address children's plight. Those who took the time to observe his service of music could neither deny the magnitude of the need nor the power of the solution. Seeing for themselves fueled their own passion and ignited their commitment to help. As J.W. said a few years before the merger, "You don't find many organizations like Hugworks that have the opportunity to make a life-changing difference." The unsolicited notes and letters from those served over the years give voice to this statement in a most compelling fashion.

To be sure, some specific events had a large bearing on the outcome. In fact, many involved in the 2015 Hugworks / KidLinks Foundation merger pointed to it as the saving event. But Celebration Shop / Hugworks had been in existence for thirty-five years prior to that action, so such a view overlooks a myriad of smaller, positive actions and relationships that helped the organization reach that point and facilitate that merger.

EVOLVE AND IMPROVE

Preserving a legacy was one of the motivations for the merger. But being considered a legacy assigns a burden that goes well beyond showing you can hang around for longer than usual. Legacy status requires setting a standard that challenges the next generation of leaders to do what they can to preserve, protect, and improve that status into the future. Everyone I interviewed for this book expressed confidence that a new generation of leaders will step forward, figure out what needs to be done, and take the necessary steps to keep the KidLinks Legacy Flywheel spinning forward.

*****

As I considered the broad sweep of the KidLinks story, I was reminded of the songs that Jim, Paul, Noel, and others wrote containing healing and helpful messages that the child in each of us can benefit from hearing. One of my personal favorites is Jim's "Circle of Friends," which expresses the importance of community. The chorus is,

Circle of friends, all holding hands Sharing our lives, all part of the plan Giving the gift that never will end We each take our place in the circle of friends

As I considered Jim's lyrics in the context of nonprofit longevity, I could see a connection to the legacy effect—where a circle of servants becomes part of the plan, each taking their place, giving their gifts with the hope that it never will end. How will you take your place in the KidLinks circle of servants?

AFTERWORD

by J. W. Brown

For more than twenty-five years, I have followed Jim Newton and his ongoing efforts to provide hope and happiness to kids. Jim, along with Paul G. Hill and Noel "Paul" Stookey, have created a fabulous library of therapeutic and uplifting music to address a full range of issues that young children and their parents may face.

I first met Jim in the late 1980s at a couples' Bible study where he provided entertainment for a group of parents and their kids. I liked the music and could tell my two daughters really enjoyed his songs. I left with a couple cassette tapes (which was how music was delivered back in the 1980s) and played them for the girls when they were sick or just needed some encouragement.

Over the next few years, I developed a meaningful friendship with Jim. In the latter part of 1999, I recognized the need for financial support to expand a fabulous library of recorded songs. I pitched the idea of holding a golf event to six colleagues. I saw it as a way to provide a networking opportunity for my energy-related colleagues while raising funds for Celebration Shop, the nonprofit platform Jim had started many years before. Jim's personal story and the music he was creating with Paul and Noel made the idea a simple sell to these guys who all had young children.

We formed the KidLinks Foundation to coordinate the golf outing, which has taken place every year since 2000. We added a chef-inspired event ten years later to raise money by providing nongolfers with a first-class dining experience. Eventually, we merged Hugworks and the KidLinks Foundation to create the current KidLinks platform. Many business partners and friends have participated in our events and, by doing so, they have enjoyed fun activities while receiving the personal benefit of doing something extraordinary for kids.

As I read this book on our history, I realized I have been truly blessed by being directly involved with KidLinks as an active sponsor of events and serving in leadership roles. Today, a great professional staff, volunteers, and an active board of directors are in place to continue making a material impact on the lives of so many kids and their families.

It has been my pleasure to be involved in the KidLinks journey and see the current nonprofit organization develop into a highly functioning one poised for continued growth. Its mission of linking kids to healing, hope, and happiness through the power of music remains a very compelling one. It is my hope that this book will encourage you to become a partner in that adventure. Believe me, you too will find it personally very rewarding.

J. W. Brown

Dallas, Texas

January 2022

ABOUT THE AUTHOR

Following his retirement as a corporate executive in 2009, Larry V. Dykstra pursued a number of experiences intended to stretch him as a person. These activities explored three broad themes: playing music with and for others, serving hospitalized children, and exploring matters of spirituality and healing. Along the way, Larry found that stringing words together on paper was a useful tool for helping him process his thoughts and find meaning.

Since 2010, Larry has spent more than seven hundred hours in children's hospitals volunteering as both a KidLinks therapeutic music entertainer and as a chaplain in the Pastoral Care Department. His 2015 book, *Musical Hugs: Succeeding through Serving, One Song at a Time*, chronicles Larry's journey from defining success in terms of what he did for a living to viewing it as what he did for others. In *Musical Hugs*, he shares stories of the positive impact that music and personal presence can have on those who are suffering. For more information, visit his website at MusicalHugs. com.

In 2016, Larry edited and published his father's World War II memoir, *In the Service of My Country: I Never Regretted a Day.* In this book, Ralph Dykstra was able to share events from the fifty missions he completed as flight engineer on a B-24 bomber more than seventy years earlier. His stories bear witness to bravery and cowardice, laughter and tears, the tragedy and triumph that accompany war. Sharing the book with hundreds of family and friends allowed the ninety-three-year-old veteran to be recognized for his role as member of the "greatest generation."

In 2025, Larry published *My Redemption from Pluto: Lessons Learned from Life's Relationships.* This book is composed of thirty-two essays which reveal lessons about the four types of relationships we all have in life – with ourselves, with others, with the world around us, and with the Divine. Larry's hope is that these stories open a pathway into each reader's personal learning journey.

As a musician, Larry is gifted with the ability to lead informal singalongs that engage audiences. He is an active member of multiple ensembles. Depending on the group, song, and audience, Larry handles a combination of rhythm guitar, mandolin, and lead or backup vocals.

To contact Larry, or to get more information about Larry and his writing, visit: authorlarryvdykstra.com.

www.ingramcontent.com/pod-product-compliance
Lightning Source LLC
Chambersburg PA
CBHW021628120626
46545CB00002B/453